32d Congress, 1st Session. | [SENATE.] | Ex. Doc. No. 100.

MESSAGE

FROM THE

PRESIDENT OF THE UNITED STATES,

IN ANSWER

To a resolution of the Senate, requesting information in regard to the fisheries on the coasts of the British possessions in North America.

August 3, 1852.
Read.
August 5, 1852.
Ordered to be printed.

To the Senate of the United States:

In answer to the resolution of the Senate, of the 23d ultimo, requesting information in regard to the fisheries on the coasts of the British possessions in North America, I transmit a report from the acting Secretary of State and the documents by which it was accompanied. Commodore M. C. Perry, with the United States steam-frigate Mississippi under his command, has been despatched to that quarter, for the purpose of protecting the rights of American fishermen under the convention of 1818.

MILLARD FILLMORE.

Washington, *August* 2, 1852.

Department of State,
Washington, August 2, 1852.

The acting Secretary of State, to whom has been referred the resolution of the Senate of the 23d ultimo, requesting the President to communicate to that body, if not incompatible with the public interest, "all correspondence on file in the executive departments, with the government of England or its diplomatic representatives, since the convention between the United States and Great Britain, of October 20, 1818, touching the fisheries on the coasts of the British possessions in North America, and the rights of citizens of the United States engaged in such fisheries, as secured by said convention. And that the President be also requested (under like limitation) to inform the Senate whether any of the naval forces of the United States have been ordered to the seas adjacent to the British possessions in North America to protect the rights of American fishermen under said convention of 1818, since the receipt of intelligence that a large and unusual British naval force had been ordered there to enforce certain alleged rights of Great Britain under said convention,'' has the honor to lay before the President the accompanying papers. These, together with those communicated to the Senate on the 28th of February, 1845, but which, it appears from the journal of that body, were not ordered to be printed, embrace all the information possessed by this department on the subject of the said resolution.

Respectfully submitted,

W. HUNTER,
Acting Secretary.

To the PRESIDENT OF THE UNITED STATES.

LIST OF ACCOMPANYING PAPERS.

Mr. Adams to Mr. Canning, (with enclosures,) June 25, 1823.
Mr. Canning to Mr. Adams, July 1, 1823.
Mr. Addington to Mr. Adams, (with enclosures,) October 12, 1823.
Same to the same, June 10, 1824.
Mr. Brent to Mr. Addington, September 8, 1824.
Same to the same, September 21, 1824.
Mr. Addington to Mr. Adams, (with enclosures,) October 5, 1824.
Same to the same, (with enclosures,) February 19, 1825.
Mr. Brent to Mr. Vaughan, February 2, 1826.
Mr. Vaughan to Mr. Clay, February 5, 1826.
Same to the same, April 29, 1826.
Mr. Bankhead to Mr. Forsyth, (with enclosures,) January 6, 1836.
Mr. Forsyth to Mr. Bankhead, January 18, 1836.
Mr. Bankhead to Mr. Forsyth, January 19, 1836.
House document No. 186, 26th Congress, 1st session.
Message from the President of the United States, referred in the report of the Acting Secretary of State as having been communicated to the Senate on the 28th of February, 1845.
Mr. Everett to Mr. Calhoun, (with enclosures,) March 25, 1845.
Same to the same, (with enclosures,) April 2, 1845.
Same to Mr. Buchanan, April 23, 1845.
Mr. Buchanan to Mr. Bancroft, (with one enclosure,) December 10, 1846.
Mr. Bancroft to Mr. Buchanan, January 4, 1847.
Mr. Crampton to Mr. Webster, July 5, 1852.
Mr. Hunter to Mr. Crampton, July 14, 1852.

Mr. Adams to Mr. Canning.

DEPARTMENT OF STATE,
Washington, June 25, 1823.

SIR: I have the honor of enclosing herewith copies of a complaint and protest received at this department, stating the capture and detention of the schooner Charles, a fishing vessel belonging to George Moody, of York, in the State of Maine, a citizen of the United States. This detention is stated to have been altogether without cause, and to have been effected by Captain Arabin of a British gun-brig called the Argus. It appears the schooner Charles has neither been restored to its owner nor carried before any tribunal for adjudication. I am directed by the President of the United States to solicit your good offices in the first instance to obtain the restitution of the schooner Charles to Mr. Moody, and in the next to claim the satisfaction and indemnity due all the sufferers by the interruption of their voyage and the disturbance in their lawful occupations, and all other damages sustained by them in consequence of these acts, to which should be added the reparation to the United States for the indignity offered to their flag and the injuries inflicted upon their citizens.

I pray you, sir, to accept the assurance of my distinguished consideration.

JOHN QUINCY ADAMS.

The Right Honorable STRATFORD CANNING,
Envoy Extraordinary and Minister Plenipotentiary from Great Britain.

Mr. Canning to Mr. Adams.

BALTIMORE, *July* 1, 1823.

SIR: In acknowledging the receipt of your official letter, dated the 25th ultimo, enclosing copies of a complaint and protest received at your department with reference to the capture and detention of the schooner Charles, a fishing vessel belonging to George Moody, of York, in the State of Maine, a citizen of the United States, I have only to mention at the present moment, that, agreeably to your request for the exertion of my good offices in the case, it will afford me pleasure to take an early opportunity of referring the papers, which you have done me the honor of communicating, to the proper authorities, for the purpose of effecting a more particular inquiry into the circumstances of George Moody's complaint and attaining the ends of justice in a spirit according with the friendly relations established between our respective countries.

I request, sir, that you will accept, on this occasion, the assurance of my distinguished consideration.

STRATFORD CANNING.

The Hon. JOHN QUINCY ADAMS,
Secretary of State.

Mr. Addington to Mr. Adams.

WASHINGTON, *October* 12, 1823.

SIR: In reference to a letter addressed by you to Mr. Stratford Canning, dated the 25th of June last, enclosing copies of a "complaint and protest received at the Department of State, stating the capture and detention of the schooner Charles, a fishing vessel belonging to George Moody, of York, in the State of Maine, and soliciting Mr. Canning's good offices, in the first instance, to obtain the restitution of the said schooner, and in the next, to claim the satisfaction and indemnity due to all the sufferers by the interruption of their voyage," to which, you subjoin, "should be added the reparation to the United States for the indignity offered to their flag, and the injuries inflicted upon their citizens," I have the honor to transmit, for your information, a copy of a letter which I have just received from the rear admiral commanding his majesty's ships on the Halifax station, covering several other documents, from various authorities, in reference to the case above mentioned.

On perusing this correspondence, you will, I trust, sir, be satisfied that the seizure and subsequent condemnation of the schooner Charles took place upon strictly legal grounds.

By the report of Captain Arabin it appears that the said schooner was found at anchor in Shelburne harbor, into which *she had not been driven by stress of weather*. From that harbor she had already sailed once, after having previously anchored there, and *had returned a second time*, before she was captured by the Argus, *the weather being fine and moderate the whole time*. She was accordingly detained by Captain Arabin, for a breach of the act 59 George III., chapter 38, passed for the protection of the British fisheries, in conformity with the stipulations of the Convention concluded between his majesty and the United States on the 20th October, 1818. On the same grounds that vessel was subsequently condemned by the vice admiralty court, at St. Johns, in the province of New Brunswick.

With regard to the equipping of the said schooner, by the captain of the Argus, and despatching her in quest of smugglers, you will observe, sir, that admiral Fahie acknowledges that act to have been irregular; but he at the same time states that irregularity to have been practised then for the first time, and announces that he has taken measures for preventing the recurrence of it.

With so frank an acknowledgment, I feel assured, sir, that you will be perfectly satisfied. The rest of the case is so clear as to render all further comment or explanation entirely superfluous.

I beg, sir, that you will accept the assurance of my distinguished consideration.

H. U. ADDINGTON.

The Hon. JOHN QUINCY ADAMS,
Secretary of State.

HIS MAJESTY'S SHIP SALISBURY,
Halifax, *September* 5, 1823.

SIR: On the 2d of last month I received a letter from Mr. Canning, dated Philadelphia, July 5, enclosing copies of a complaint and protest given in to the government of the United States by an individual named George Moody, a citizen, as he is described, of the United States, relative to the detention of the American schooner "Charles," by his British Majesty's sloop the "Argus," and requesting me to afford him such information respecting the case as would enable him to place it in a proper light.

Previously to my receipt of Mr. Canning's letter, Captain Arabin, who commanded the Argus when the detention of the schooner occurred, had returned to England—a circumstance which obliged me to draw from other sources the particulars of her detention, and of the subsequent proceedings in the vice-admiralty court at New Brunswick, which have been followed by her condemnation.

Mr. Canning's departure for Europe causes me to avail myself of the intimation of your appointment as chargé d'affaires *ad interim*, contained in his letter to me of the 24th of June, to forward for your information and that of the American government, copies of several documents, as particularized at the foot of this letter, which go to contradict, in material points, the statements made in the protest, and will, I trust, sir, furnish sufficient evidence that the Charles was detained and proceeded against on legal grounds.

The manning, however, and sending her "down the bay in pursuit of smugglers," which is admitted in the report of Mr. Innes, the first lieutenant of the Argus, was certainly irregular; and, if she had been acquitted, it would probably have induced the court to award a proportional remuneration to the claimants. It is the first instance of such a proceeding that has come within my knowledge, and I have taken measures to prevent its recurrence.

I have the honor to be, &c.,

W. C. FAHIE,
Rear Admiral and Commander-in-Chief.

HENRY U. ADDINGTON, Esq.,
His British Majesty's Chargé d'Affaires.

Copies of documents above referred to.

No. 1. The commander of the Argus's letter, enclosing statements, &c., relative to the detention of the American schooner Charles.

Nos. 2, 3, 4. Statements of officers of the Argus relative thereto.

No. 5. Extract from the Argus's log-book for the 9th of May, the day of the detention of the Charles.

No. 6. Letter from the collector of his Majesty at St. John's, New Brunswick, stating the condemnation of the schooner Charles on the 17th of July, in the court of vice admiralty there.

No. 7. Memorandum of Captain Arabin's reasons for detaining the Charles, as given in to the customs at St. Johns, and enclosed in the collector's letter, No. 6.

W. C. F.

No. 1.

His Majesty's sloop Argus,
Halifax, August 11, 1823.

Sir: In compliance with the orders contained in your letter of the 6th instant, I have called upon the officers of his Majesty's sloop Argus, under my command, who had anything to do with the seizure and detention of the schooner Charles, American fishing vessel, and I beg leave to enclose for your information a detail of the circumstances of this case, as delivered to me by the respective officers; as also an extract from the Argus's log-book of the 9th of May, 1823.

I have the honor to be, &c.

JOHN B. DUNDAS, *Commander.*

To Rear Admiral Fahie, C. B.,
Commander in Chief.

No. 2.

His Majesty's Sloop Argus,
Halifax, August 11, 1823.

Sir: In compliance with your order to make known to you such particulars as I may be acquainted with, relative to the schooner Charles—American fishing vessel—I beg leave to state, that, having been ordered by Captain Arabin, on the 9th of May, 1823, to board the said schooner, lying in Shelburne harbor, I went in the gig, manned by four seamen and the corporal of marines, and, having boarded, demanded her papers. I inquired what brought him *within* the *limits?* And the master replied, to avoid a storm. How long he had been at anchor? He replied, he had but just anchored. I then ordered the master to weigh; and, according to the orders I had received from Captain Arabin, anchored close to the Argus. I was ordered on board, and to bring the master and schooner's papers with me.

I am, sir, &c.,

HENRY TROUCH, *Midshipman.*

Captain John B. Dundas,
His Majesty's Sloop Argus.

No. 3.

His Majesty's Sloop Argus,
Halifax, August 10, 1823.

Being ordered by Captain Arabin, on the 9th of May, to take charge of the American schooner Charles and proceed along the coast to St. John's, New Brunswick, and detain such unlawful vessels as I might meet in my way, I sailed from Shelburne on the 12th of May, and, on my way to St. John's, detained one English and one American schooner, and arrived at St. John's on the 20th of May, at which place I was taken out of the schooner Charles and she was delivered into the custom-house.

H. LEGARD, *Midshipman.*

No. 4.

His Majesty's sloop Argus,
Halifax, August 11, 1823.

Sir: In obedience to your orders to make known to you such particulars as I may be acquainted with relative to the American schooner Charles, I beg leave to state that on the arrival of his Majesty's sloop Argus, at Shelburne, on the 9th of May, 1823, the Charles was at anchor in that port, and was boarded by Mr. Henry Touch, (midshipman,) and brought to an anchor close to the Argus, by Captain Arabin's order. She was detained in the usual way, but I am not acquainted with the circumstances of her detention. I believe it was owing to information received from the shore of her having committed some breach of the treaty.

On the Argus sailing on the 12th of May, she was given in charge of Mr. Legard, midshipman, to proceed to St. John's, New Brunswick, and the crew, their clothes and provisions, with the exception of the master, were, at their own request, taken on board the Argus for a passage to St. John's. The master afterwards requested that his brother might accompany him in the Charles, which was granted. They were landed with their clothes at St. John's, New Brunswick, on the Argus's arrival on the 16th of May.

On the 20th, the Charles arrived and was reported to the collector of the customs for libelling. On the 21st she was manned and given in charge of Mr. Hugh Bowers, midshipman, and sent down the bay in quest of smugglers; when the master requested a passage, he was taken on board and landed at Campo Bello, about two miles distant from Moose island, (United States;) on the 7th of June the Charles again joined the Argus, and was ordered to St. John's, where she was given up to the collector of his Majesty's customs for legal adjudication.

I am, sir, &c.,
D. B. INNES,
First Lieutenant his Majesty's sloop Argus.

Captain John Dundas,
His Majesty's sloop Argus.

No. 5.

Extract from the log-book of the proceedings of his Majesty's sloop Argus, Septimus Arabin, esq., captain.

H.	K.	F.	Courses.	Winds.	Signals.	Remarks, &c.—Friday, 9th of May, 1823.
1–5		At anchor in Liverpool harbor		NE	E. P.	A. M.—Moderate and hazy weather. At 4, light winds and fine weather. At 5.40, got under weigh and made sail; unbent the main-top-gallant sail to repair, and bent another. At 8, moderate breezes and cloudy; Hope Island W. by S. ½ S.; Matson N. by E. ½ E. At 8.30, set the studding sails. At 10, in ditto, and hove to; hoisted out the 2d cutter, and sent her in shore, through the Ragged Islands, to examine some small vessels at anchor. Bore up, 10.30; hove to, and sent the gig in shore to examine vessels; bore up for Shelburne harbor. At noon, moderate and cloudy; opened a cask of beef.
6–8		Running along shore	SW. ½ S.			
9	4-4		W. by S. ½ S.		D. B. S.	
10–12		Running for Shelburne			W. N. T.	
1–2		Running into Shelburne harbor				Bearings and distance: Bell Rock N. by W. ½ W., ¼ mile; light-house W. by S.
3–12		At anchor in Shelburne harbor		SE. by E.		P. M.—Moderate breezes and cloudy. At 12.30, boarded and detained an American fishing vessel, the Charles. At 1.20, shortened sail and came to, with the small bower, in Shelburne harbor; Sandy Point ENE. 1¼ mile; Shelburne NNE.; a red store-house E. ¼ N. At 4, fresh breezes and cloudy. Our boats returned with two American fishing vessels detained by them. At 8, fresh breezes and cloudy. At midnight, moderate and cloudy.
					E. P.	
					D. B. S.	
				SE.		
					W. N. T.	
					E. P.	

EDWARD POTTER, *Master*.

No. 6.

CUSTOM HOUSE,
St. Johns, N. B., August 23, 1823.

SIR: I have this moment had the honor to receive your letter of the 13th inst., stating that a complaint and protest of George Moody, master of the American fishing schooner Charles, had been transmitted to you by his Majesty's envoy extraordinary in the United States, respecting the seizure of that vessel by his Majesty's sloop Argus; and of Captain Arabin having employed the said schooner as a cruizer; and you request me to give you all the information on these subjects in my power.

I accordingly beg leave to refer you to the enclosed copy of a paper transmitted to me by Captain Arabin on his arrival in this port, dated the 16th of May last, which contains a full detail of the cause of seizure, under which she was subsequently libelled in the vice-admiralty court here and condemned on the 17th of July last.

As to that part of the complaint of Captain Arabin having manned and employed the schooner to cruize, I have no knowledge of that circumstance and am inclined to think it is incorrect.

I have the honor to be, &c.,
H. WRIGHT, *Collector.*

W. C. FAHIE, Esq., C. B.,
Rear Admiral and Commander-in-chief, Halifax.

No. 7.

MEMORANDUM *of particulars of seizure by the Argus of the American fishing vessel Charles, on the south coast of Nova Scotia.*

The American fishing schooner Charles, William Stover master, belonging to York, state of Maine, detained by the Argus at Shelburne on Friday, 9th of May, 1823, for a breach of the act of 59 Geo. III, chapter 28, for the protection of the British fisheries, and to enable his Majesty to make regulations respecting the same, according to a convention made between his Majesty and the United States, 20th October, 1818. The said schooner was found at anchor in Shelburne harbor, into which she had not been driven by stress of weather or any other fortuitous circumstance. Information had been received of this schooner having put into that same harbor on the Tuesday previous to the seizure, and anchored below Sandy Point, *the weather being fine and moderate at that time, as well as on the day of seizure.* She went out on Wednesday and *returned again on Thursday,* where she was found by the Argus on Friday; and *having remained hovering* upon the coast instead of proceeding on her fishing voyage, when there was no pretence whatever for her putting into port, she was detained.

SEPTIMUS ARABIN.

His Majesty's sloop Argus, at St. John's, N. B., May 16, 1823.

Mr. Addington to Mr. Adams.

WASHINGTON, *June* 10, 1824.

SIR: In reference to the subject of a letter which I had the honor to address to you on the 12th of October last, namely, the detention by Captain Arabin of his Majesty's ship Argus, and illegal employment as a British cruizer of the American fishing schooner Charles, on which subject I subsequently, in pursuance of instructions from home, gave you verbally the assurance "that orders would be issued by his Majesty's government, that any American vessel detained by the Charles while thus irregularly employed, should be restored to the owner, even although liable on other grounds to be condemned;" I have now the honor to inform you that an inquiry having been instituted into this subject by orders of the admiralty, it has been found that only one American vessel, the Dolphin, was detained by the Charles previous to her adjudication, and that the requisite intimation for the restoration of that vessel has been made to the proper authorities, in conformity with the assurance thus given to the United States government on the part of his Majesty's ministers.

I have the honor to be, with distinguished consideration, sir, your most obedient humble servant,

H. U. ADDINGTON.

To Hon. JOHN QUINCY ADAMS, &c., &c.

Mr. Brent to Mr. Addington.

DEPARTMENT OF STATE,
Washington, September 8, 1824.

SIR: I have the honor to transmit to you three memorials from sundry citizens of the United States, belonging to the State of Maine, accompanied by seven protests and affidavits which exhibit the nature and extent of the facts referred to by the memorialists, complaining of the interruption which they have experienced during the present season in their accustomed and lawful employment of taking and curing fish in the Bay of Fundy and upon the Grand Banks, by the British armed brig Dotteril, commanded by Captain Hoare, and another vessel, a provincial cutter of New Brunswick, acting under the orders of that officer; and earnestly soliciting the interposition of this government to procure them suitable redress. With this view, I was charged by the Secretary before his late departure from this city, to communicate to you the above papers, and to request your good offices towards obtaining for the sufferers the indemnity to which they appear to be so well entitled, not only from the peculiar nature and extent of the injuries and losses of which they complain, proved and illustrated as they are by the series of protests and depositions accompanying their memorials, but from the serious violation of the rights and liberties of the citizens of the United States which they involve in the use of the same fisheries; and I have the honor, accordingly, to request that you will have the goodness to make such representations to the commanding officer of the naval forces of your government on that station, or to the Colonial government of New Brunswick, as may be available, not only for the relief of the memorialists, but for the prevention of similar interruptions in future.

I have the honor to be, with distinguished consideration, sir, your obedient and very humble servant,

DANIEL BRENT.

Henry U. Addington, Esq.,
Chargé d'Affaires from Great Britain.

Mr. Brent to Mr. Addington.

Department of State,
Washington, September 21, 1824.

Sir: I have the honor to transmit to you copies of some additional papers* which have been received at this office, upon the subject of the interruption, likewise given by the same armed British brig Dotterel, to vessels of the United States, employed in the prosecution of the fishery in the bay of Passamaquoddy, and elsewhere in the same neighborhood, as particularly exemplified in the cases of the two schooners, William and Rebecca, which are fully stated in the enclosures, and to pray the interposition of your good offices in behalf also of the owners of these vessels, towards obtaining for them the indemnity to which they may be justly entitled.

I have the honor to be, with high consideration, sir, your obedient and humble servant,

DANIEL BRENT.

Henry U. Addington, Esq.,
Chargé d'Affaires from Great Britain.

Mr. Addington to Mr. J. Q. Adams.

Washington, *October* 5, 1824.

Sir: I have the honor to acknowledge the receipt of two letters, one dated the 8th and the other the 21st ultimo, which Mr. Brent addressed to me, in pursuance of instructions from you, relating to certain American fishing vessels averred to have been detained, in violation of the terms of the convention of 1818, by his Majesty's sloop Dotterel in the bay of Fundy in the months of June and July last.

I shall not fail to communicate, without loss of time, the whole of the papers relative to this matter, to the admiral commanding his Majesty's naval forces at Halifax, and in so doing shall strongly recommend that a full and impartial investigation be made into the merits of the various cases therein reported; the result of which shall be forthwith imparted to you, whenever it comes to my knowledge.

Mean time, sir, I must inform you that a report of those very occurrences, of a nature very different from that made by the individuals to you, has reached me from rear-admiral Lake, of whose letter, together with its enclosures, I have the honor to transmit to you copies herewith.

---

* The papers here referred to cannot be found on the files of the Department of State.

It is therein made to appear that the fishing vessels above mentioned were detained by the Dotterel solely on account of their having been detected in the commission of a direct infraction of the treaties existing between the two nations, having in fact been found pursuing their occupation without the boundaries assigned to them by the terms of the convention of 1818.

On this point, however, the parties are at issue, each stating his case according to his own view of it. Thus far, therefore, there is ground for a candid and impartial investigation on both sides. Such I have recommended to Admiral Lake, and such, I trust, you will also cause to be instituted here.

But there is another point, sir, on which I lament that there should be no ground for doubt or hesitation as to the course which I have to pursue.

By a perusal of the enclosed documents you will perceive that after the detention of the Reindeer and Ruby by the master of the Dotterel, and while on their way to St. Andrews, "an attack was made on three vessels by two schooners and an open boat, *under American colors, full of armed men, with muskets and fixed bayonets,* amounting to about one hundred, headed by a Mr. Howard of Eastport, who is said to be a captain in the United States militia, in consequence of which the master thought it most prudent to surrender to such superior force."

This, sir, is an outrage of such a nature as to leave me no other alternative than to make a formal demand from the American government for the infliction of punishment on the offenders.

Whether the vessels were legally detained or not, such an act of violence will bear no justification. If individuals are permitted to expound the stipulations of treaties for themselves, with arms in their hands, the preservation of harmony and good understanding between nations can no longer be hoped for.

I am disposed—no person can be more so—to act fairly and openly by the citizens of this republic, whenever they have just ground of complaint against British authorities, and shall accordingly take every measure for ascertaining whether the detention of the vessels in question was legal or not.

If it was not legal, you have abundant proof, sir, in your own hands, of the disposition of his Majesty's government to afford the most prompt and equitable redress to the parties aggrieved. I allude to the case of the American schooner Charles, detained and employed as a tender last year by his Majesty's sloop Argus. That act, you will recollect, was condemned as illegal by his Majesty's ministers, and restitution ordered to be made to the parties who suffered through the exercise of it, although otherwise liable, by the illegality of their conduct, to the entire loss of their property.

But in the mean time, sir, it becomes my duty to demand reparation, by the punishment of the transgressors, for the act of violence perpetrated on persons bearing his Majesty's commission, while engaged in the discharge of their public duties.

I feel confident, sir, that you will view this outrage in the same light as myself, and consider such conduct equally dangerous to the peace and well-being of the two countries, and I have no doubt that you will see the expediency of causing immediate proceedings to be instituted against the principal actors in this disgraceful scene.

I beg, sir, that you will accept the renewed assurances of my distinguished consideration. H. U. ADDINGTON.

HALIFAX, *September* 9, 1824.

SIR: I have the honor to transmit to you a copy of a letter, dated the 26th ultimo, from Captain Hoare, of his Majesty's sloop Dotterel, with its enclosure from Mr. John Jones, master of that sloop; also copies of two letters from Captain Hoare, dated the 2d instant, one of them containing a copy of the affidavit therein mentioned.

By the first of these communications you will perceive that two American vessels, called the Reindeer and Ruby, were seized by the master of the Dotterel in Two Island Harbor, Grand Manan, on the 26th of July, for a breach of the treaty between Great Britain and the United States; and that on the evening of the same day, when abreast of harbor De Lute, proceeding to St. Andrews, an attack was made on the vessels in question by two schooners and an open boat, under American colors, full of armed men, with muskets and fixed bayonets, amounting to about one hundred, having the appearance of militia men, and headed by Mr. Howard, of Eastport, who is said to be a captain in the United States militia; in consequence of which the master thought it most prudent to surrender to such superior force.

Captain Hoare's next letter mentioning his having, on the 29th ultimo, on his passage to Halifax, fallen in with the American schooner Madison, (by her papers Ansel Coggens, master,) which he was informed was one of the vessels to which the men belonged who rescued the before-mentioned vessels from his master, and that, finding on board this vessel a man named David Rumney, whom one of the marines of the Dotterel identified as one of the persons concerned in the rescue, Captain Hoare thought proper to detain the vessel and take Rumney on board the Dotterel as a prisoner.

Captain Hoare's other letter refers to the Pilgrim, an American fishing vessel, seized by him at Grand Manan in June last, for a breach of the treaty, which vessel was afterwards rescued by some of her crew, in conjunction with one of the men whom Captain Hoare had put in charge of her; and the said vessel having been fallen in with on the 29th ultimo, and a man named Winslow, who Captain Hoare was informed was one of those actively engaged in the forcible rescue of the said vessel, she was taken possession of and the man (Winslow) put on board the Dotterel as a prisoner.

As in these transactions his Majesty's officers have been assaulted in the execution of their duty by armed subjects of the United States, and the property of which they had in his Majesty's name taken lawful possession rescued from them, in violation of the treaty subsisting between Great Britain and the United States, I consider it necessary that the subject should be brought officially before the American government, in order that steps may be taken to prevent the continuance of such proceedings, and therefore request you will be pleased to adopt such measures on the occasion as shall appear to you to be necessary.

I have the honor to be, &c.,

W. T. LAKE,
Rear Admiral and Commander-in-Chief.

H. U. ADDINGTON, Esq.,
His Majesty's Charge d'Affaires.

HIS MAJESTY'S SLOOP DOTTEREL,
August 26, 1824.

SIR: I have the honor to enclose the copy of a letter from the master of his Majesty's sloop under my command, detailing the circumstances of his having been attacked off Campo Bello by two armed schooners, under American colors; and that two American fishing vessels he had detained were taken from him and carried into Eastport.

I have the honor, &c.,

RICHARD HOARE, *Commander.*

REAR ADMIRAL LAKE,
Commander-in-chief, &c., &c., Halifax.

HIS MAJESTY'S SLOOP DOTTEREL'S BOAT,
St. Andrew's, N. B., July 27, 1824.

SIR: I beg leave to represent that on 25th instant, when cruising in the yawl, in pursuance of your orders, off the Grand Manan, for the protection of our fisheries, I received information of several American fishing vessels being at anchor at Two Island harbor, and that two of them, namely, Reindeer and Ruby, of Lubec, were at White Island harbor on the 24th, where they got their wood and water, and that on their anchoring they fired their muskets and told the inhabitants they were armed, and would not allow any man-of-war's boat to board them, and after they had their supplies they shifted to Two Island harbor, Grand Manan.

I made sail from Gull cove, and at daylight, the 25th, observed four schooners at anchor at Two Island harbor, which vessels got under weigh on our appearing; when I got close to three of them they lashed along side each other, and all hands, about thirty in number, went on board the middle one with their fire-arms and fish spears. I desired them to separate, which they refused to do until I threatened to fire on them. On boarding, they proved to be the Reindeer, master's name Small, and Ruby, master's name Small, (brothers,) of Lubec, two fishing vessels, and Friend's shallop, of the same place.

It being fine weather, and they not being in want of wood or water, I detained the Reindeer and Ruby, and put their men, with the exception of the masters, on board the two American schooners with provisions for a passage to Lubec, and made sail in the Reindeer and Ruby for St. Andrews through East Quady. About 6 p. m., when abreast of Harbor De Lute, I observed two schooners and an open boat full of armed men, muskets and fixed bayonets, hoisting American colors; one of them went along side

Mr. Towneau in the Ruby, boarded and took the arms from him and his three men; the one abreast of me was kept off for about a quarter of an hour, when they commenced firing into us. Though with great reluctance I thought it most prudent to surrender to such superior force, having but four men, one musket and three cutlasses.

On delivering them up, I found there were in the two schooners about a hundred armed men, (including the crews of the schooners, about thirty in number,) the rest having the appearance of militia men, and headed by a Mr. Howard, of Eastport, said to be captain in the United States militia.

I have the honor to be, &c.,

JOHN JONES, *Master.*

To Captain Hoare,
His Majesty's Sloop Dotterel.

His Majesty's Sloop Dotterel,
Halifax, September 2, 1824.

Sir: I have the honor to inform you that while running past the outer bank of the Grand Menan, on the 29th ultimo, on my way to this port, I fell in with the Pilgrim, American fishing schooner, taken by one of my boats on the 16th of June, at Grand Menan, for infringing the treaty, but was retaken by the crew, aided by John Martin, one of the two men put in charge of her. I have taken possession of and ordered her to this port. Enclosed, sir, is a copy of an affidavit made by William Paine (marine) and the other man in charge of the Pilgrim, on their arrival at Lubec, by which affidavit you will see, sir, that a man by the name of Winslow, one of the crew of the Pilgrim, was the most active person in retaking her, and that he forced the cutlass from William Paine, and obliged him to go below. Under these circumstances I felt I should be justified in considering him a prisoner, and as such he now remains on board the Dotterel. That he ought to be punished in some way that may deter others of his nation from committing the same offence under similar circumstances, I am sure, sir, you will think necessary. I have therefore to request you will be pleased to solicit the advice of the attorney-general on this important point, that I may be governed thereby in my proceedings.

I have the honor to be, &c., &c.,

RICHARD HOARE, *Commander.*

Copy of the Enclosure in the foregoing Letter.

William Paine, one of the marines belonging to his British Majesty's brig Dotterel, maketh oath and saith: That on Wednesday last the American fishing-boat Pilgrim was seized for a violation of the treaty between the United States and Great Britain, and the deponent, with James Martin, seaman, put on board to take charge of her. That on the night of the 21st instant, between the hours of eleven and twelve, it being Martin's watch, he, this deponent, was awoke from sleep by the roll of the vessel; that he attempted to go on deck, but found the companion doors shut. This deponent then broke open the companion doors, armed himself and went on deck, and ordered Captain Woodward, the master of the boat, then at the helm, to put the boat about; he refused. Martin was rowing; this deponent went forward and ordered him to drop the oar, but he would not, till this deponent threatened to cut his head off if he did not. While the deponent was thus endeavoring to get the vessel about, Winslow and Martin suddenly sprung upon him and obliged him to go below. This deponent was then brought to the place in the said boat Pilgrim, against his will, and against all the exertion in his power to make.

his
WILLIAM × PAYNE.
mark.

Benjamin Scott, one of the hands on board the Pilgrim, on oath saith: That the foregoing statement of Mr. William Paine is, according to his best knowledge and belief, substantially true. That he was below when Mr. Paine armed himself and went on deck, and soon after he returned and said he had been overpowered and his arms taken from him. That the Pilgrim was taken by Woodward and Winslow, aided by Martin, to Lubec. This deponent further saith, that Woodward and Winslow both acknowledge that Mr. Paine discharged his duty to the utmost of his power; that superior force alone caused him to surrender his arms.

BENJAMIN SCOTT.

STATE OF MAINE,
Washington county, } *ss:*

To all to whom these presents may come: Know ye that on the 27th day of June, A. D. 1824, before me, Sol. Thayne, notary public by legal authority, duly commissioned and sworn, and residing at Lubec, personally appeared the aforenamed William Payne and Benjamin Scott, and made solemn oath that the delarations by them personally made and signed were just and true.

In testimonium veritatis.

SOL. THAYNE, *Notary Public.*

NEW BRUNSWICK,
Charlotte county, } *ss:*

I, the undersigned, one of his Majesty's justices of the peace in and for said county, residing in Campo Bello, do hereby certify that on the 23d day of June, 1824, William Paine, the person in the annexed instrument mentioned, appeared before me and declared the facts therein contained, which appear to me to be correct. That Solomon Thayne is a notary public for the county of Washington, in the State of Maine, United States, duly appointed, and that full faith and credit may be given to his attestation.

D. OWEN, *Justice of the Peace.*

HIS MAJESTY'S SLOOP DOTTEREL,
Halifax Harbor, September 2, 1824.

SIR: I have the honor to inform you that while running past the outer bank of the Grand Menan on the 29th ultimo, on my passage to this place, I fell in with the Madison, American fishing schooner, (by her papers, Cozzens, master,) and as I was informed by Winslow, one of the crew of the Pilgrim, American fishing vessel, and who was then on board the Dotterel, that she was one of the schooners that attacked the master off Harbor de Lute on the 26th July, and the master having affirmed that the name of the vessel that attacked him was the Madison, though he cannot swear to the vessel, as all that description of vessels are so much alike, but he believes her to be the same, and on the crew coming on board the Dotterel, one of them, Daniel Rumney, was immediately recogised by William Vickery, one of the mariners in the boat with the master, as being one of those who were in and took an active part in the vessel that attacked them, and on boarding the said Madison it was discovered the master had left her, and as she had her boat out I have no doubt he had gone on board one of the other fishing vessels to escape detection, as he would have been immediately recognised by the master; and as some dates on the back of the papers relative to her arrival and leaving Lubec at different periods, prove her to have been at Lubec about the time of the master having been attacked; those circumstances together, left no doubt in my mind of her being the Madison that, with another schooner named the Diligence, attacked the master off Harbor de Lute on the 26th July, and I therefore took possession of her and ordered her to this port. As it appears to me, sir, that this circumstance of two armed schooners attacking, and taking from a British officer and British crew two vessels he had legally detained, is an act of piracy, and all those concerned therein ought to be punished.

I have for the present detained Daniel Rumney on board, and I have to request you will be pleased to solicit the advice of the attorney general on this important subject, that I may be guided thereby in my proceedings relative to the said Daniel Rumney.

I have the honor to be, &c., &c.,

RICHARD HOARE, *Commander.*

Rear Admiral LAKE,
Commander-in-Chief, &c., &c., &c.

Mr. Moody to Mr. Adams.

YORK, MAINE, *June* 12, 1823.

SIR: I would refer you to the enclosed protest for the particulars of an outrage committed on my property by the commander of a British brig, and pray that you would lay the same before the proper authorities that measures may be immediately taken to restore to me my property.

I am, respectfully, sir, your obedient servant,

GEO. MOODY.

Hon. JOHN Q. ADAMS,
Secretary of State, Washington.

By this public instrument of declaration and protest, be it known that William Stover, of York, in the county of York and State of Maine, mariner, and late master or skipper of the schooner called the Charles, of York aforesaid, of the burden of forty tons or thereabouts, owned by George Moody, of said York, merchant; and Josiah Stover, Solomon Avery, Theodore Webber, jr., William Simpson, jr., and Hanson Forgerson, all of York aforesaid, fishermen, employed and engaged on board said schooner for the present fishing season, personally appeared and came before me, Alexander McIntire, notary public within and for the county of York and State of Maine, who did on this tenth day of June, in the year of our Lord one thousand eight hundred and twenty-three, severally solemnly protest and declare, allege and affirm that having previously engaged with the said George Moody, the owner of said schooner Charles, to go in her for the present fishing season, and said vessel being fitted out in York with all things necessary to prosecute said fishing voyage and under fishing license, we sailed from said York on the 4th day of May last past on our said voyage, and in prosecution of our said voyage we sailed to the coast of Nova Scotia and came to anchor for the first time after leaving York, about eight leagues south-south-east from Shelburne on said Nova Scotia coast, on Thursday the 8th day of May, at which place we lay till Friday morning, May 9th, at about nine o'clock. The wind blowing very fresh from the ESE. and a heavy sea, we found that we could no longer lay at anchor, but found that we were drifting fast to leeward, and fearing an approaching storm, which actually took place the following day, we were obliged to put into Shelburne for a harbor to avoid the winds and seas. We caught sixty-eight codfish and three herring only while we lay at anchor as before mentioned, which were all the fish we caught after we left York. We got into Shelburne about 12 o'clock at noon on the same day and came to anchor. About an hour after we came to anchor in Shelburne, the British gun-brig called the Argus, which, as we were told, was commanded by Captain Arabin, hove in sight and soon after came into Shelburne and came to anchor, having previously sent her barge manned with an officer and six men to us, who boarded us, took possession of our schooner and ordered us to heave up our anchor immediately and go alongside of the British brig. The master or skipper was ordered to go on board said brig with the schooner's papers, and after being detained on board said brig about a quarter of an hour was sent on board the schooner again, having had his papers taken from him. The boat was taken from off our deck and carried alongside the said brig the same day. We lay alongside said brig till Monday, the 12th day of May, when four of our crew, namely, William Simpson, jr., Theodore Webber, jr., Solomon Avery and Hanson Forgerson, were taken from the schooner and put aboard the said brig; and two officers and seven men were put aboard the schooner, and the said master or skipper and Josiah Stover were kept on board said schooner. The officers and men put on board said schooner were armed with small arms and cutlasses, victualed for twenty days.

The brig proceeded to St. John's, where she landed the said William Simpson, jr., Theodore Webber, jr., Solomon Avery and Hanson Forgerson, destitute of money or clothing, excepting what clothing they had on their backs. We, the said William Stover and Josiah Stover, further protest, affirm and declare, that we were detained on board the said schooher Charles on a cruise of nine days in the Bay of Fundy; during which cruise she took two fishing vessels belonging to the United States and carried them into St. John's, and was there again victualed for another cruise of twenty days; and after laying one day at St. John's she then sailed on her second cruise, and on the 22d day of May last we were landed from said schooner at Campo Bello, where all the fishermen's clothes were given up to the said master or skipper.

We further declare and say, that after we sailed from York, on the 4th day of May, as before named, till we were boarded and taken possession of by the said brig Argus, no person was on board our said schooner, except our said crew, nor were any of the said crew of said schooner on shore at any place, and our boat was not taken from our deck after leaving York till it was taken off by order of the officers of the brig Argus, nor was any article taken out of said schooner, from the time we left York till she was taken possession of as before named.

Therefore the said William Stover and his said crew, to-wit: Josiah Stover, Theodore Webber, jr., William Simpson, jr., Solomon Avery, and Hanson Forgerson, did declare and protest, as by these presents they do most solemnly protest, against the commander and crew of the said brig Argus, and against every person concerned in the capture of said schooner Charles, for arbitrarily, unlawfully, unjustly and cruelly taking said schooner, as no just or legal cause existed to justify said taking and detention.

WILLIAM STOVER,
THEODORE WEBBER, jr.,
WILLIAM SIMPSON, jr.,
JOSIAH STOVER,
SOLOMON AVERY,
his
HANSON × FORGERSON.
mark.

STATE OF MAINE, *York, ss:*

The within named William Stover, Theodore Webber, jr., William Simpson, jr., Josiah Stover, Solomon Avery and Hanson Forgerson, personally appeared before me, Alexander McIntire, notary public within and for the county of York, and entered the foregoing public declaration and protest by them severally subscribed, and made solemn oath that all the facts therein stated by them severally are true.

In witness whereof, I have hereunto subscribed my name and affixed my [L. S.] notarial seal, this 10th day of June, in the year of our Lord one thousand eight hundred and twenty-three.

ALEXANDER McINTIRE,
Notary Public.

A true copy from the original. Attest:

ALEXANDER McINTIRE,
Notary Public.

Mr. Addington to Mr. Adams.

WASHINGTON, *February* 19, 1825.

SIR: On the 8th and 21st of September last, I had the honor of receiving from the Department of State two letters, in which my good offices were requested in behalf of certain individuals of the State of Maine, engaged in the fishing trade, who desired redress and reparation for injury done to them by the seizure of their vessels by his Majesty's sloop Dotterel, while employed in cruizing on the coasts of his Majesty's North American possessions.

I informed you, sir, in reply to those communications, that I should forthwith address an application to the British naval commander-in-chief on the North American station, recommending that a full and impartial investigation should be instituted into the various cases which formed the grounds of complaint on the part of the American government.

I have the honor to transmit to you herewith, copies of a correspondence which took place in consequence of my application, between Captain Hoare, commanding his Majesty's sloop Dotterel, and Rear-Admiral Lake, in reference to the cases set forth in your letters above mentioned. The depositions of the officers and men concerned in the capture of the vessels* therein enumerated are also annexed.

By a perusal of these documents it will, I trust, sir, most conclusively appear to you that the complainants have no just ground of accusations against the officers of the Dotterel, nor are entitled to reparation for the loss they have sustained; that, on the contrary, they rendered themselves, by the wilful irregularity of their own conduct, justly obnoxious to the severity exercised against them, having been taken, some *flagrante delicto*, and others in such a position and under such circumstances as rendered it absolutely impossible that they could have had any other intention than that of pursuing their avocations as fishermen within the lines laid down by treaty as forming the boundaries within which such pursuit was interdicted to them.

With regard to the charge preferred against Captain Hoare, of his having converted detained American vessels, prior to their adjudication in the courts, into tenders for assisting him in his operations against the vessels of the same country, I have only to observe that that officer broadly and in the most explicit terms denies ever having committed or authorized one such act. And in respect to the other accusation addressed by the complainants, of maltreatment by the British officers of those persons whose vessels had been detained, I trust that a perusal of the enclosed papers will make it equally clear to you that that charge is entirely unfounded.

I cannot but apprehend, sir, that the acrimony with which the proceedings of Captain Hoare have been viewed by the citizens of the State of Maine, employed in the fishing trade on the British North American coasts, may be justly ascribed to the circumstance of the recent substitution of vigilance, on the part of the British cruizers, for the laxity which appears to have prevailed heretofore in guarding those coasts from the intrusion of foreign fishermen and smugglers; and I doubt not that if those persons could be prevailed upon to confine themselves within the limits prescribed

---

*Rebecca, Ruby, Reindeer, William, Galeon, Pilgrim, Hero.

to them by the treaty, no cause of dissension or complaint would ever arise between the individuals or vesssels of the two nations.

It remains for me to observe that, in one case in which, by the ignorance of the midshipman employed in the service, the territory of the United States had been violated, by the pursuit and seizure of an American vessel within the American boundaries, Captain Hoare made all the reparation in his power for his officer's misconduct, by delivering up to the Americans the boat which had been detained, and paying all the expenses incident to her detention.

I have the honor to be, with distinguished consideration, sir, your most obedient, humble servant,

H. U. ADDINGTON.

The Hon. JOHN QUINCY ADAMS, &c., &c., &c.

HIS MAJESTY'S SLOOP DOTTEREL,
Halifax, November 25, 1824.

SIR: According to your direction, I have made the strictest investigation and enclose the reports of Mr. Jones, master, and Mr. Brotheroe, mate, also the testimony of the several men belonging to their boats, relative to the several American fishing vessels they had seized, which I trust will be sufficient proof of the propriety of detaining these vessels; and as the American fishermen do not keep any journal or log, there cannot be possibly any proof but the crews of the boats detaining them and the Americans. It is not to be supposed that the latter will acknowledge to have violated the treaty existing between the two governments relative to the fisheries. I think you will perceive a consistency throughout the several reports of Messrs. Jones and Brotheroe that will bear the stamp of truth. Why should they detain these vessels if they had not violated the laws? it could not be for their value, for they had little or nothing in, and they knew if they were condemned and sold they would sell for a mere trifle—the best of them not more than forty dollars; there were many other American fishing vessels of much more value which they might have seized if it was merely to annoy them or for the sake of what they might sell for; but it is known every where in the Bay of Fundy that the American fishermen have invariably made use of the several harbors in the Manan, as if these islands formed a part of the United States; they come in and haul their nets, and there are many instances of their having cut away the nets of the islanders, and I was informed by the fishermen at the Manan, previous to my leaving the Bay of Fundy, that they had taken treble the quantity of fish this year to that of any preceding year since the war, and they ascribed it entirely to the American fishermen having been kept without the distance prescribed by treaty, (three marine miles from the shore.)

The former cruizers in the Bay of Fundy, (*vide* Captain Arabin's letter, dated his Majesty's sloop Argus, off Bermuda, December 17, 1822,) have not paid much attention to the fisheries off Manan, and consequently the American fishermen have gone into the harbors whenever they pleased, and being more numerous than the inhabitants, have overawed them; but I have been informed by some of the fishermen resident there, that more than once they have had it in contemplation to represent the conduct of, and the injury they have sustained from the American fishermen, but their living remote from each other, and no educated persons among them, they have been at a loss how to draw up a petition, or who to apply to for redress.

As all the vessels alluded to in the papers sent by Mr. Addington were taken by the boats, I cannot myself make any observations on their capture, but shall confine myself to a few remarks on the protest of the American fishermen, and to answer the complaint you have called my particular attention to.

Why do not the crews or owners of the American fishing vessels detained for violating the treaty, come forward when the vessels are adjudged in the vice-admiralty court and produce such evidence as would clear them? They say to claim their vessels in the vice-admiralty court of New Brunswick would be total loss. The fact is it would not answer their purpose so well; they are well aware that witnesses could be produced that would falsify their testimony; the fishermen at the Manan would immediately come forward to witness the fact of their being in their harbors and drawing their nets when not in want of an article of provision or fuel; but the Americans are aware that when their protest comes before the commander-in-chief of this station, the vessel of war will have left the Bay of Fundy, and that there will remain but the testimony of the officer and boat's crew that detained them, which they will take care to outnumber. If the vice-admiralty courts of New Brunswick are conducted illegally and wrong, should they not make a representation to the British government, that they may be better conducted? How is the captain of a man-of-war stationed in the Bay of Fundy to act, if the proceedings in the vice-admiralty court are to be considered illegal and void, merely from the protest of some American fishermen?

What are the vice-admiralty courts instituted for but to try causes and decide whether the capture is just, and I should conceive that when they have passed judgment, the captain of the seizing vessel is released from further responsibility: sufficient time is allowed all parties to procure and produce evidence, and if they do not come forward, is it not a tacit acknowledgment of the badness of their cause? and such is the case with these American fishing vessels; they have asserted many things that are wholly false. It is stated in memorial A, "that nine sail of American fishermen have been captured and sent into the province of New Brunswick, while others have been converted into tenders without trial, for the purpose of molesting our fishermen; they have insulted and abused the crews; turned them on shore in a foreign country entirely destitute, and without the means of returning to their homes."

That any American fishing vessel detained by the Dotterel or her boats has been converted into a tender for the better molesting their fishermen is wholly false; that the crews have, to my knowledge, been insulted and abused, must be a gross and wilful perjury; it had always been the custom, I understand, to allow the crews of the vessels detained to take their clothes and such provisions as they pleased and find their way to the States. I have sometimes offered to carry them back when I returned to Passamaquoddy; they have invariably been allowed to take away everything they could claim as their private property, and the whole of their provisions on board their vessel, with which they paid their passage back to their country.

And in the memorial C it is said, "that the American fishermen have no occasion nor inducement to violate the provisions of the aforesaid convention, nor have they, as we firmly believe, given, in any instance, just cause of complaint."

It is a well known fact that the American fishermen leave their fishing ground every Saturday (when there is not a man-of-war, or her boats, in the neighborhood) and anchor in some of the harbors of Manan until the Monday, bringing in the fish offal with them and throwing it overboard on the inner banks, by which they drive the fish off those banks; and they haul their nets during the Sunday and catch sufficient bait for the ensuing week. This they suppose is not known—for they are not ignorant that this is a violation of the provisions of the convention; the fact is they want, by causing much trouble, to deter the man-of-war stationed in the Bay of Fundy from interfering with them at all.

That the brig's barge has come into the wharf at Eastport, and taken and carried away two boats laden with flour, Lieutenant Driffield's letter on that subject will, I think, completely invalidate that charge.

That the Hero—American fishing vessel—captured on the 16th of June, has not been sent in for trial, but is armed and is still used as a tender to the Dotterel, is entirely false. She was not used by me to annoy a single American vessel, and on her arrival at St. John's was delivered over to the collector of the customs, and ought, long ere this, to have been adjudged in the vice-admiralty court.

"That the officers having charge of the armed boats of the Dotterel, ordered to cruise round Grand Manan and Campo Bello, have written instructions, which have been exhibited, to seize and send into St. Andrew's all American fishing vessels found within three marine miles of the said island."

My order to the officers of the boat has been, that any American vessels they may find within three marine miles of the shore, except in evident cases of distress, or in want of wood or water, they are to detain and send or carry them to St. Andrew's.

I have the honor to be, &c.,

RICHARD HOARE, *Commander.*

Rear Admiral LAKE,
Commander-in-Chief, &c., &c.

HIS MAJESTY'S SLOOP DOTTEREL,
Halifax, November 8, 1824.

SIR: I beg leave to represent, in obedience to your orders of this day's date, directing me to give a statement of the facts, and under what circumstances I detained the American fishing schooner at different anchorages at the Grand Manan, while cruizing in the yawl, in pursuance of your orders, for the protection of our fisheries, that on the second of July last, on boarding an English vessel, I found a man named Wright officiating as pilot to carry her to Grau harbor, who told me he belonged to the American fishing schooner Rebecca, then at anchor at Woodward's cove, and that they came there for water. Satisfied with his assertion, I continued cruising, and shortly after I observed the American vessel getting under weigh, leaving the said man (Wright) behind. I ran down towards her; they not heaving to, after I had fired several shots across their bow, I chased her over to the Nova Scotia shore, where I lost sight of her. On the 6th following, I found the said American schooner Rebecca at anchor, cleaning fish and throwing the offal overboard, and the aforesaid man (Wright) on board. It being fine weather, and they having three barrels of water on board, with a sufficient quantity of wood, I detained her and took her to St. John's.

On the 15th of the same month I found the American fishing schooner William anchoring in Gull cove; the weather was fine until after she got in, when it came on foggy, with light breezes, and they having two barrels of water on board, which myself, Mr. Tongeau and boat's crew subsequently used from, and plenty of wood, I detained her. Having found the American schooner Rover, of Addison, (Crowly master) landing a great part of her cargo of green fish to a Mr. Fowler, of Gull cove, I made the William's boat fast to the yawl for the night, to prevent their crew from doing the same. As for their getting water, about sunset, and a vessel to anchor alongside of them, Mr. Tongeau and I know it to be impossible, as I had a sentry planted on shore, about two cables' length from them, and if they received any water after dark, it was done as a pretext, for the boat's crew were witnesses to the water I found on board when I first boarded her; and that I threatened to confine the master to the deck, and lash a pump brake across his mouth, as stated in their protest, that is false. On my first boarding her, with only three men, in a small boat, they were very abusive to us, and one of them said if they were all of his mind they would heave that fellow overboard—pointing to me. I told him if he did not keep quiet I would lash him to the deck.

At three p. m., same day, (15th) I received information from the fishermen at Gull cove, as well as from the master and crew of the fishing schooner Minerva, of Grand Manan, that an American schooner was at anchor at Beal's passage. I went out from Gull cove and saw her there; at nine o'clock in the evening I boarded her, which proved to be the American fishing schooner Galeon, and found all the crew asleep. On questioning the master the reason of his being there, he told me he had come to throw the gurry (offal of the fish) overboard. They not being in want of wood or water, and a fine fair wind for them, I detained her, got her under weigh, and ran for Gull cove, a direct course for their fishing ground. What the crew of the last mentioned vessel asserted in their protest is not true. I never said that I would release their vessel, but told them that it was not in my power to do it, as they had decidedly violated the treaty of convention between England and the United States; but as they pleaded poverty, saying their vessel was their sole support, I told them I would recommend their case to Captain Hoare, of the Dotterel, my commanding officer. Both schooners, William and Galeon, I took to St. Andrew's next day.

On the 25th of the same month I received information from the master and crew of the fishing schooner Industry, of Grand Manan, that several American fishing schooners were at anchor at Two Island harbor, and that two of them, namely, the Reindeer and Ruby, of Lubec, were at White Island harbor on the 24th, where they got their wood and water; and that, on their anchoring there, they told them and the inhabitants they were armed, and would not allow any man-of-war's boat to board them; and after they had their supplies they shifted to Two Island harbor. At daylight, on the 26th, observed four schooners at anchor at Two Island harbor, which got under weigh on our appearing. When I got close to three of them they lashed alongside each other, and all hands, thirty in number, went on board the middle one, with fire-arms and fish-spears. I desired them to separate, which they refused to do, until I threatened to fire on them. On boarding them they proved to be the Reindeer, Ruby, Friends and Diligent, American fishing schooners. It being fine weather, and they not in want of wood or water, I detained the Reindeer and Ruby, and by the sanction of the masters of the Diligent and Friends, I put the crews of the Reindeer and Ruby on board of them, with as much provision as they wished to take, and on our passage to St. Andrew's, the said schooners, Reindeer and Ruby, were forcibly taken from me by armed vessels under American colors, as stated in my letter of the 27th July last.

I have the honor to be, &c., &c.

J. JONES,
Master of H. M. sloop Dotterel.

RICHARD HOARE, *Commander.*

HIS MAJESTY'S SLOOP DOTTEREL,
November 9, 1824.

SIR: In obedience to your orders I herewith add a statement of the Pilgrim and Hero, American fishing schooners:

On the 16th of June last I observed these schooners laying off the Grand Menan, and upon approaching them one of the schooners got under weigh and stood in for the shore; 3 30 p. m. observed the schooner under weigh, heave her lines overboard and haul in fish, the schooner then within one and a half mile of the island; 3 40, fired and brought to the schooner; 3 45, boarded the Pilgrim, then about one mile or one mile and a quarter from the shore; she had on board fish alive; took possession of her for a breach of the treaty; I then took to the N. ½ E. and boarded the Hero, who had made sail from in shore, whilst I was on board the Pilgrim, and finding she was in want of nothing, I inquired what she had been doing so near the shore with her sails down; to which I was informed by one of the crew they had been cleaning their fish on shore; in consequence of which, and having seen her within one mile of the land, I took possession of her also; stood in and anchored in Two Island harbors. Thursday, the 17th, being for the most part of the day calm, I remained at anchor.

Friday, the 18th, at 7 a. m., weighed and stood for Beaver harbor; from 9 to 12 calm; 3 p. m. observed two schooners under the Eastern Wolf, then about one mile distant; it being calm at the time, I ordered the master of the Pilgrim to send me her small boat, not having one myself—upon receiving which I ordered one of my seamen and one marine armed into her; the boy who brought the boat I told to remain on board until I returned, but on his expressing a wish to go, and knowing he was more acquainted with her than any of my men could be, I agreed that he should pull, and ordered my seamen on board, part of the way I pulled, and part of the way the marine pulled with the boy; when I returned, there being no appearance of wind, I ordered the schooners Pilgrim and Hero to follow me and anchor under the Eastern Wolf for the night.

Saturday, the 19th, it being calm, I did not weigh until 11 a. m., then a light breeze; stood for Beaver harbor, where I anchored at 3 p. m., with an intention of waiting the Dotterel; arrived, therefore, unbent sails, and caused the Pilgrim and Hero to do the same.

Sunday, the 20th, 11 20 a. m., observed the Dotterel pass in the offing to the eastward, bent sails, and observed the Pilgrim and Hero to do the same; 12 20 p. m. weighed, schooners in company, beat out of the harbor, but finding the Pilgrim and Hero could not, I bore up, stood in and anchored, schooners in company

Monday, the 21st, at 7 p. m. weighed, with light airs, schooners in company; beat up and anchored in Mason's bay at 8 30 p. m.

Tuesday, the 22d, at 2 30 a. m. the sentry reported one of the schooners was gone.

Wednesday, the 23d, fresh gales until 10 a. m., then light airs with heavy rain—still at anchor.

Thursday, the 24th, at 9 a. m., weighed with light airs, and stood for Point la Pro, Hero in company; but falling calm, was obliged to fall into Dipper harbor.

Friday, the 25th, heavy rains with strong breezes from the eastward; remained at anchor.

Saturday, the 26th, weighed, but were obliged to put back again.

Sunday, the 27th, weighed, and ran up to St. John's.

I further beg leave to state that I did detain on board the crews of the Pilgrim and Hero, having no authority for acting otherwise; that Winslow, in Beaver harbor, said he was aware of having fished within the limits, and if I would allow him and crew to go home he would give up his schooner and never again ask for her. Part of the men were at times on board my boat and living the same as my boat's crew, who had the allowance of the British navy excepting spirits, which had been all used, to make up for which I gave from my private stock to those of the schooners who were on board my boat. I never asked them to do any duty on board my boat, nor did I at any time make use of harsh or menacing language; the duty done by the persons taken out of one or either of the schooners was a perfect voluntary act of their own; the arms spoken of were taken from the Pilgrim, through expressions made use of by Winslow, for safety: powder, a quarter of a pound; shot, about one pound; the arms were delivered to the gunner, the papers of each schooner were delivered to the custom-house at St. John's.

I have the honor to be, &c., &c., &c.,

S. R. BOTHUS, *Mate.*

R. Hoare, *Commander.*

Evidence of Mr. Towneau, midshipman, and the crew of the yawl boat belonging to her Majesty's sloop Dotterel, relative to the detention of the American fishing schooner William.

Mr. Towneau, midshipman, examined relative to the detention of the American schooner William.

Question. Were you in the yawl when Mr. Jones detained the American schooner William?

Answer. Yes.

Q. State the particulars.

A. Mr. Jones sent me with James Lloyd, marine, on a point of land to look out. We saw two or three vessels working up; observed one of them anchor in Gull cove. Mr. Jones went out in the small boat to board her; he hailed us to come along side in the yawl, which we did, and found Mr. Jones had detained her. We then took their fish knives from them, having heard by some people both on shore and on board some English vessels that they would oppose us in boarding. We unbent her sails and took them with us in the yawl; also her boat.

Q. Do you know Mr. Jones' reason for taking her boat?

A. Yes; to prevent her crew going on shore to exchange fish for rum, knowing that another American fishing vessel had done the like with Mr. Fowler at Gull cove the same day; also to prevent their getting water, as the American fishermen generally make that a pretext for coming in.

Q. What quantity of wood and water had she on board?

A. I cannot say the exact quantity, but there was sufficient for her crew and ours to carry her to St. Andrew's, at which place we did not arrive till several days after her detention.

Q. How was the weather?

A. Very fine with a moderate breeze: but after she anchored it came on foggy.

Thomas Richardson examined.

Question. Were you in the yawl with Mr. Jones when he detained the American schooner William?

A. Yes.

Q. Relate all you know respecting her.

A. I went with Mr. Jones in the small boat to board her; went below and overhauled what quantity of wood and water she had on board.

Q. What quantity of wood and water had she?

A. About sixty gallons of water below and thirty on deck, and about a cord and a half of wood.

Q. How was the weather?

A. The weather was moderate and hazy, but after she anchored it came on foggy.

James Lloyd, marine, examined:

Question. Were you in the yawl when Mr. Jones detained the American schooner William?

Answer. I cannot recollect the vessel's name, having detained several.

Felix Shaw, marine, examined:

Question. Were you in the yawl when Mr. Jones detained the American schooner William?

Answer. Yes.

Q. Relate the circumstances you know about her.

A. I cannot recollect any of the particulars, as we detained several.

John Cammish, seaman, examined :

Question. Were you in the yawl when Mr. Jones detained the American schooner William?

Answer. Yes.

Q. Relate what you know of the circumstances.

A. It is so long since, I cannot recollect the particulars.

Richard Newland, seaman, examined :

Question. Were you in the yawl with Mr. Jones when he detained the American schooner William?

Answer. Yes.

Q. Relate what you know respecting her detention.

A. When we fell in with the William she was laying in Gull cove. Mr. Jones asked what they were doing there. They said they came in for wood and water. Mr. Jones detained her, unbent her sails, and took them with us on shore in the yawl, and likewise took their small boat with us.

Q. Do you know the reason why Mr. Jones unbent her sails?

A. To prevent her, I believe, from going to sea during the night.

Q. What quantity of wood and water had she on board?

A. About three barrels of water and a cord of wood.

Q. How was the weather?

A. Fine weather with a light breeze.

Q. Do you know the position of the fishing-ground?

A. I do not know the bearing of it by compass, but I could see the vessels at anchor on the fishing ground.

Q. Was the wind fair for going on it?

A. Yes, it was.

Q. Were you in the small boat when Mr. Jones boarded her?

A. Yes, I was.

Q. Did you hear the master of the vessel assign any reason for coming in there?

A. He said they came in for wood and water.

William Vickery, marine, examined :

Question. Were you in the yawl when Mr. Jones detained the American schooner William?

Answer. Yes, I was.

Q. Relate what you know respecting her detention.

A. I observed a schooner come in and anchor within a mile of the shore. Mr. Jones went out to board her, and brought her in the cove and anchored.

Q. Were you on board the schooner?

A. Yes.

Q. What quantity of wood and water had she on board?

A. I know there were two barrels, but cannot say whether there was any more; was not down in the hold, and cannot say what wood there was.

Q. How do you know it was the William?

A. I saw the William of Addison on her stern.

John Lloyd, seaman, examined:

Question. Were you in the yawl when Mr. Jones detained the American schooner William?

Answer. Yes, I was.

Q. Relate the particulars.

A. I was with the greater part of the crew encamped on a point of land; observed a schooner come in and anchor. She was boarded, but cannot recollect whether it was by Mr. Jones or Mr. Towneau.

Q. Were you on board the schooner?

A. Yes, I was. I went off and assisted in unbending the sails.

Q. Do you remember what quantity of wood and water she had on board?

A. I do not perfectly recollect the quantity, but there was one cask handed up half full which they said they were going to get filled on shore, but were prevented by Mr. Jones.

Q. Did you hear any of the crew say their reasons for coming in?

A. Yes; for wood and water.

Q. How was the weather?

A. Fine weather, and a fresh breeze.

John Cheese, seaman, examined:

Question. Were you in the yawl with Mr. Jones when he detained the American schooner William?

Answer. Yes, I was.

Q. Relate all you know about her.

A. I was sick in a tent on shore, and do not know any of the particulars.

William Payne, marine, examined:

Question. Were you in the yawl with Mr. Jones when he detained the American schooner, William?

Answer. Yes.

Q. Relate all you know of the particulars.

A. I went on board with Mr. Jones in the small boat to examine her. Mr. Jones detained her; unbent her sails, and took them on shore.

Q. Do you know what wood and water she had on board?

A. I cannot say.

Q. Did you drink any of the water on board of her?

A. Yes, I did.

Q. How was the weather?

A. Fine, with a strong breeze.

We, the undersigned, have examined the aforesaid persons, belonging to his Majesty's sloop Dotterel, taking the minutes of their depositions respecting the detention of the American fishing schooner William; and we do declare that their evidence has been taken in a very impartial manner, and that the persons aforesaid have not been biassed in any way whatsoever.

JOHN COOKE,
Senior Lieutenant H. M. Sloop Dotterel.
JAS. HAZZARD,
Purser H. M. Sloop Dotterel.

Evidence of Mr. Towneau, midshipman, and the crew of the yawl boat belonging to his majesty's sloop Dotterel, relative to the detention of the American fishing schooner Galeon.

Mr. Towneau examined:

Question. Were you in the yawl when Mr. Jones detained the American schooner Galeon?

Answer. Yes, I was.

Q. Relate the particulars respecting her detention.

A. While at Gull cove Mr. Jones went out one evening in a small boat to cruize. About 11 p. m. Mr. Jones returned with an American schooner which he had detained. Next morning about 8 o'clock Mr. Jones sent me on board the Galeon to take charge of her. About 9 o'clock we got under weigh, and made sail for St. Andrew's.

Q. Do you know Mr. Jones's reason for detaining her?

A. I believe for their having broken the treaty; but do not know the particulars, as I was left on shore in charge of the yawl.

Q. How was the weather?

A. I believe it was a fine, clear night.

Q. What quantity of wood and water had she on board?

A. I cannot state the quantity, but we used from it some days after her detention.

Q. How was the wind?

A. From the northward, and I think north by west.

Thomas Richardson examined:

Question. Were you in the yawl with Mr. Jones when he detained the American schooner Galeon?

Answer. Yes.

Q. Relate what you know respecting her detention.

A. I went in a small boat with Mr. Jones, and pulled out of Gull cove; boarded two English schooners, who informed us that an American schooner was laying under the land, which vessel we boarded, and found the crew below, asleep. Mr. Jones asked them what they came in for. Their reply was, for wood and water, and that they had got it that afternoon. Mr. Jones then asked them their reason for not going away. They said they were waiting for wind and tide. He then got her under weigh, and ran her to Gull cove, which place lay between us and the fishing ground.

Q. Do you know the position of the fishing ground?

A. Yes, I could see it from Gull cove.

Q. Was the wind fair for the Galeon to proceed to the banks?
A. Yes, it was.
Q. Do you know the passage from Gull cove to the fishing banks?
A. Yes; a clear passage outside the Black Kedge towards the banks.
Q. What kind of weather was it?
A. Very fine and clear, with moderate breezes.
Q. What quantity of wood and water had the Galeon on board?
A. I do not know the quantity, but observed three or four casks and a quantity of wood.

WILLIAM PAYNE, marine, examined:

Question. Were you in the yawl with Mr. Jones when he detained the American schooner Galeon?
Answer. Yes.
Q. Relate the particulars respecting her detention.
A. I went with Mr. Jones in a small boat in the afternoon, (the day of the month I do not remember,) and boarded an English schooner, where we were informed an American fishing schooner was laying under the land. We boarded her, and found the crew all below. Mr. Jones asked them their reason for being there. They replied they came in for wood and water. He then asked them why they did not go away when they had got it. They said they were going at daylight. He detained the schooner and took her to Gull cove, and on the following morning got under weigh for St. Andrew's.
Q. Do you know the position of the fishing banks?
A. Yes; I could see the vessel on the banks.
Q. Was the wind fair for the Galeon to proceed to the banks?
A. Yes; for the banks lay nearly in a line with Gull cove from where we detained the Galeon.
Q. On what quarter was the wind when you ran towards Gull cove?
A. Very near before the wind. We came close to the cove, and then we hauled up into the cove.
Q. How was the weather?
A. Fine clear weather and fresh breezes.
Q. What quantity of wood and water had the Galeon on board when detained?
A. She had two casks of water on deck, and a great quantity of wood.

FELIX SHAW, marine, examined:

Question. Were you in the yawl with Mr. Jones when he detained the American schooner Galeon?
Answer. Yes.
Q. Relate the particulars.
A. I was one of the crew of the small boat that went out with Mr. Jones. In the afternoon (the day of the month I do not recollect,) boarded an English schooner near Gull cove, who said that we had better keep a good look-out or we should get a good handspiking from the American schooner then lying in shore. We shortly after boarded the American

schooner Galeon. Mr. Jones asked them what they were doing there. They said they came in for wood and water, and had got it that afternoon. Mr. Jones asked them, if they had their wood and water, why they had not gone to sea. Their reply was they did not think it worth while to go to sea that night; and the master requested Mr. Jones to let him go that time, and he would not come in again. We then got under weigh, and took her to Gull cove for that night. One of the crew was very abusive. We afterwards carried her to St. Andrews.

Q. Do you know the position of the fishing grounds?

A. No, I do not.

Q. How was the wind when you ran for Gull cove?

A. A fair wind, and fine, clear weather.

John Lloyd, seaman, examined:

Question. Were you in the yawl with Mr. Jones when he detained the American schooner Galeon?

Answer. Yes.

Q. Relate the particulars respecting her detention.

A. When at Gull cove we observed a schooner run in and anchor. We boarded her in the small boat, which proved to be English. They told us that the Galeon American fishing schooner was laying at an anchorage then about three miles off. We then left the English schooner and boarded the Galeon. I was left as boat-keeper, and cannot state what passed on board. Shortly after she was got under weigh, and ran to Gull cove. One of the crew of the Galeon was very abusive to us. She was afterwards taken to St. Andrew's by Mr. Jones.

Q. Do you know the position of the fishing ground?

A. No, I do not.

Q. How was the wind for Gull cove?

A. A fair wind.

Q. How was the weather?

A. Fine clear weather.

Q. What quantity of wood and water had the Galeon on board?

A. I do not know.

James Lloyd, marine, examined:

Question. Were you in the yawl with Mr. Jones when he detained the American schooner Galeon?

Answer. I was in the yawl when he detained some American fishing schooners, but cannot recollect their names.

John Cammish, seaman, examined:

Question. Were you in the yawl with Mr. Jones when he detained the American schooner Galeon?

Answer. Yes.

Q. Relate what you know respecting her..

A. It is so long since that, I cannot recollect any particulars.

RICHARD NEWLAND, seaman, examined:

Question. Were you in the yawl with Mr. Jones when he detained the American schooner Galeon?

A. Yes.

Q. Relate what you know respecting her detention.

A. I was left in a tent on shore at Gull cove, and recollect Mr. Jones going out in a small boat and bringing the Galeon into Gull cove.

Q. How was the weather?

A. Fine weather, with a light breeze.

Q. Did you ever go in the Galeon to St. Andrew's?

A. Yes.

Q. Do you know what quantity of wood and water she had on board?

A. She had four casks of water and about two cords of wood.

JOHN CHEESE, seaman, examined:

Question. Were you in the yawl with Mr. Jones when he detained the American schooner Galeon?

Answer. Yes.

Q. Relate all you know respecting her detention.

A. I cannot state the particulars, as I was sick in a tent on shore.

WILLIAM VICKERY, marine, examined:

Question. Were you in the yawl with Mr. Jones when he detained the American schooner Galeon?

Answer. Yes.

Q. Relate what you know respecting the detention.

A. I was left on shore in the tent; Mr. Jones went out in the small boat and brought the Galeon in the evening.

Q. How was the weather?

A. Fine weather.

Q. Were you one of the crew that took the Galeon to St. Andrew's?

A. Yes.

Q. What quantity of wood and water had she on board?

A. Two casks of water on deck and one in the hold, and plenty of wood.

We, the undersigned, have examined the aforesaid persons belonging to his Majesty's sloop Dotterel, taking the minutes of their depositions respecting the detention of the American fishing schooner Galeon, and we do declare that their evidence has been taken in a very impartial manner, and that they have not been biassed in any way whatever.

JOHN COOKE,
Senior Lieutenant H. M. Sloop Dotterel.
JAMES HAZZARD,
Purser H. M. Sloop Dotterel.
RICHARD HOARE,
Commander.

Evidence of the crew of the Dotterel's tender relative to the detention of the American fishing schooners, Hero and Pilgrim.

William Payne, marine, examined:

Question. Were you in the Dotterel's tender with Mr. S. R. Protheroe when he detained the American fishing schooners Hero and Pilgrim?

Answer. Yes.

Q. Relate the particulars respecting their detention?

A. I first saw the Pilgrim about two miles from the land, fishing; made the best of our way to close her, and boarded her, having live fish on her deck. Mr. Protheroe asked them what business they had to fish in our waters? They replied they thought it was not in our waters. Mr. Protheroe then said, I shall detain you and take you to St. John's. I was directed by Mr. Protheroe to take charge of the Pilgrim, with another seaman, and to follow him. I afterwards observed the tender board another schooner, which proved to be the Hero.

Q. What distance was the Hero from the land when Mr. Protheroe boarded her?

A. About two miles.

Q. State what followed after leaving the Manan.

A. We anchored at Beaver harbor with the Hero and tender, and afterwards proceeded the same day and anchored in Mason's bay. Late one evening Mr. Protheroe sent us our evening's grog, and having the middle watch, I went below and laid down on the lockers to sleep. In the middle of the night I was awoke by the motion of the vessel, and endeavored to get on deck but could not, as the companion hatch was secured down against me. I then forced it open, and went on deck and found the vessel under weigh, in the possession of the Americans. The seaman with me refusing his assistance I was obliged to submit, and was forcibly carried to Lubec, where they allowed me to go on shore. From thence I made the best of my way to St. John's, and rejoined the Dotterel.

Q. Did you at any time hear Mr. Protheroe make use of any abusive language to the Americans?

A. No.

Q. Did you hear or know that Mr. Protheroe at any time compelled the Americans to assist in working the vessel?

A. No; but they did assist with their own free will.

John Donovan, seaman, examined:

Question. Were you in the Dotterel's tender with Mr. Protheroe when he detained the American schooners Hero and Pilgrim?

Answer. Yes.

Q. Relate all the particulars you know relative to their detention.

A. We fell in with the Pilgrim while running into the Manan. I think she was about a mile and a half from the land. Saw them hauling up fish, and on boarding her found live fish on her deck. Mr. Protheroe said he should detain her for fishing in our waters. He sent two men on board to take charge. We then made sail for another schooner, which proved to be the Hero. When we boarded her she was about a mile and a half from the land, with lines overboard fishing, and had live fish in the hold. Mr.

Protheroe asked them what they had been doing close in shore with the sails down. A man named Winslow said they had been cleaning fish on shore. I was sent on board the Hero with another man to take charge and to follow the tender and Pilgrim, which we did, anchoring each night until our arrival in Mason's bay, at which place the Pilgrim made her escape in the night. We afterwards proceeded, anchoring each night till we arrived at St. John's.

Q. What quantity of wood and water had the Hero on board?

A. Two casks of water and some wood; the quantity I cannot say.

Q. Did you at any time hear Mr. Protheroe make use of abusive language to the Americans?

A. No, I did not.

Q. Did Mr. Protheroe compel any Americans to work?

A. No, not to my knowledge, but they continued assisting the working of the vessel with their own free will.

THOMAS CASSADY, seaman, examined:

Question. Were you in the Dotterel's tender with Mr. Protheroe when he detained the American schooners Hero and Pilgrim?

A. Yes.

Q. Relate the particulars.

A. We were running in for the Manan and boarded the Pilgrim, American schooner, about a mile or a mile and a quarter from the land, fishing. Mr. Protheroe asked what business they had fishing there, as they were within three miles of the land. The answer was they did not know they were within the limits. Mr. Protheroe detained her and put two men on board to take charge, and we proceeded to board another schooner which proved to be the Hero, about two miles from the land.

Q. Did you hear Mr. Protheroe ask the master of the Hero if he could assign any reason for being so near the land with her sails down?

A. Yes, but did not hear the reply.

Q. What became of the Hero?

A. Mr. Protheroe sent two men on board her to take charge, and we proceeded to Mason's bay, anchoring each night in the tender, with the Hero and Pilgrim in company, at which place the Pilgrim made her escape in the night; afterwards we proceeded to St. John's in the tender, with the Hero, where she was delivered over to the customs.

Q. Did you at any time hear Mr. Protheroe use any abusive language to the Americans?

A. I did not.

Q. Did Mr. Protheroe compel the Americans in the tender to work?

A. No, he did not; but they sometimes voluntarily assisted in working the tender.

Q. Did you at any time know Mr. Protheroe to put the Americans on one meal a day, or know them to fare worse than the tender's crew?

A. No, we all messed alike, having the allowance of the British navy, excepting spirits for part of the time, which was all used, and I know Mr. Protheroe to have frequently given them rum from his own private stock.

OMAS RUSSELL, seaman, examined:

Question. Were you in the Dotterel's tender with Mr. Protheroe when detained the American schooners Hero and Pilgrim?

Answer. Yes.

Q. Relate all the particulars.

A. In running from Grand Passage to Grand Manan observed two schoon- lying at anchor, one of which got under weigh and stood in shore. We de the best of our way to close her. I observed her with lines overboard ing. We then boarded her, which proved to be the Pilgrim, American ing schooner. She had at the time live fish on her deck. Mr. Pro- roe detained her and put two hands on board to take charge, she then ng within a mile of the shore. Observed another schooner make sail from shore from the northward; stood for her, fired, brought to and boarded American fishing schooner Hero. Mr. Protheroe then asked the master at they had been doing in shore, a man named Wilson said, "we have n on shore cleaning fish." Mr. Protheroe detained her. On our way St. John's anchored under the Eastern Wolves; as we were going in ob- ved two schooners about a mile aft of us; Mr. Protheroe hailed the Pil- m for the boat, which was brought to us in the tender by a boy who uested Mr. Protheroe to be allowed to pull him on board the aforesaid ooners; Mr. Protheroe with a man and the boy proceeded to board these sels. We then with the Hero and Pilgrim proceeded for St. John's, choring each night till we arrived at Mason's bay when the Pilgrim ected her escape during the night; afterwards we proceeded in the ten- , Hero in company, to St John's, when the hero was delivered up to the stom-house.

Q. Did you at any time hear Mr. Protheroe make use of abusive language the Americans?

A. No.

Q. Did you at any time hear Mr. Protheroe threaten to ill use or mal- at the Americans on board the tender?

A. No, I did not.

Q. Did Mr. Protheroe compel the Americans to work in the tender?

A. No, but they did sometimes assist voluntarily.

Q. Did you at any time know Mr. Protheroe to put the Americans on e meal a day, or know them to fare worse than the tender's crew?

A. No, Mr. Protheroe never interfered about the prisoners, and we all ssed alike, having the established allowance of the British navy, except- g spirits for part of the time, which had been all used, and I know Mr. otheroe to have frequently given them rum from his own private stock.

SAMUEL GOODANEW, marine, examined:

Question. Were you in the Dotterel's tender with Mr. Protheroe when detained the American schooners Hero and Pilgrim?

Answer. Yes.

Q. Relate all the particulars respecting that detention.

A. In standing over from Grand Passage to Grand Menan, observed two hooners at anchor, one of which got under weigh and stood in shore; ade the best of our way and boarded the Pilgrim about two miles from the land to the best of my judgment. I did not go on board her, but she was detained by Mr. Protheroe and two hands put on board to take charge. We then made sail and boarded the Hero, then about a mile and a half from the shore. Mr. Protheroe inquired what they had been doing in shore with their sails down; a man by the name of Wilson said they had been on shore cleaning their fish. Mr. Protheroe detained her and put two hands on board to take charge. Proceeded, anchoring each night, to the Eastern Wolves; in going in observed two schooners about two miles from us; took the Pilgrim's small boat and boarded them. Mr. Protheroe, myself and the American boy who brought on board the boat, who was allowed to go by his own request. We then proceeded to Mason's bay, anchoring each night, with the Hero and Pilgrim in company, at which place the Pilgrim got away during the night. We afterwards proceeded to St. John's with the Hero in company, which vessel was delivered to the custom-house at that place.

Q. Did you at any time hear Mr. Protheroe make use of any abusive language to the Americans?

A. No, I did not. I must have heard it had it taken place, as I never left the tender.

Q. Did Mr. Protheroe compel the Americans in the tender to work?

A. No, they sometimes assisted with their own account.

Q. Did you at any time hear Mr. Protheroe threaten to ill use or maltreat the Americans on board the tender?

A. No, I did not; but must have heard it had it happened.

Q. Did you at any time know Mr. Protheroe to put the Americans on one meal a-day, or to fare worse than the tender's crew?

A. No, we messed all alike, having the established allowance of the British navy excepting spirits, which we drank during the bad weather. I know Mr. Protheroe to have given them spirits from his own stock. I was the person who attended Mr. Protheroe, and gave the spirits to them myself by his direction.

JOHN WAKE, marine, examined:

Question. Were you in the Dotterel's tender when Mr. Protheroe detained the American schooners Hero and Pilgrim?

Answer. Yes, I was.

Q. Relate all the particulars respecting their detention.

A. In running from Grand Passage to the Grand Manan observed two schooners lying at anchor, one of which got under weigh and stood in shore, which vessel was chased; observed her fishing and hauling live fish in; boarded her, which proved to be the American schooner Pilgrim. She had at the time live fish on her deck. Mr. Protheroe detained her and put on board two hands to take charge of her, she then being about two miles from the shore to the best of my judgment. We then chased another schooner, which had made sail from in shore; boarded her, then about a mile and a half from the land; proved to be the Hero, American fishing schooner. Mr. Protheroe asked them what they were doing in shore: a man by the name of Wilson said they had been on shore cleaning their fish. Mr. Protheroe detained her and put two hands on board in charge of her. We then proceeded with the schooner to Mason's bay, anchoring each night, when the

Pilgrim made her escape in the night; we then proceeded to St. John's in the tender with the Hero in company, at which place she was delivered over to the custom-house.

Q. Did you at any time hear Mr. Protheroe make use of any abusive language to the Americans on board the tender?

A. No, I did not.

Q. Did Mr. Protheroe compel the Americans in the tender to work?

A. No, he did not; they helped to work the tender by their own accord.

Q. Did you know Mr. Protheroe ill use or maltreat the Americans on board the tender?

A. No.

Q. Did you know him to put the Americans on one meal a-day, or fare worse than the tender's crew?

A. No, they eat and drank with us: we had the established allowance of the British navy, except spirits part of the time, which had been used during the bad weather. I recollect once Mr. Protheroe giving them a part from his own private stock.

—

John Cole, seaman, examined:

Question. Were you in the Dotterel's tender with Mr. Protheroe when he detained the American schooners Hero and Pilgrim?

A. Yes.

Q. Relate all the particulars you know respecting their detention.

A. When running from Grand Passage to the Grand Manan, observed a schooner about two miles from the land, fishing. We boarded her, which proved to be the Pilgrim, American fishing schooner. I saw live fish on her deck. Mr. Protheroe detained her, and put two hands on board to take charge of her: we then made sail and boarded another schooner, the Hero. Mr. Protheroe detained her also.

Q. Do you know what Mr. Protheroe detained her for?

A. No, I do not; I did not hear any questions put, as I was getting my clothes to go on board the Hero. We then made sail, in company with the tender and Pilgrim, and proceeded to Mason's bay, at which place the Pilgrim effected her escape during the night. We afterwards went to St. John's with the tender and Hero in company, at which place the Hero was delivered over to the custom-house.

—

We, the undersigned, have examined the aforesaid persons belonging to his Majesty's sloop Dotterel, taking the minutes of their depositions respecting the detention of the American fishing schooners Hero and Pilgrim; and we do declare that their evidence has been taken in a very impartial manner, and the persons aforesaid have not been biassed in any way whatever.

JOHN COOKE,
Senior Lieut. H. M. Sloop Dotterel.
RICHARD HOARE,
Commander.

Evidence of Mr. Towneau, midshipman, and the crew of the yawl boat belonging to her majesty's sloop Dotterel, relative to the detention of the American fishing schooners Reindeer and Ruby.

Mr. TOWNEAU examined:

Question. Was you in the yawl with Mr. Jones when he detained the American schooners Reindeer and Ruby?

Answer. Yes.

Q. Relate all the particulars relative to that detention.

A. I recollect while in Gull cove of having received information on a Sunday from some men and a Mr. Franklin, that several American fishing vessels were at anchor in White Head harbor, and that they anchored there the evening before; that on their anchoring one of them fired three muskets and said they were armed and manned, and would oppose our boarding them. I acquainted Mr. Jones with the information I had received, who went immediately in the small boat to cruize, and returned in the evening. He told me that he had boarded an English fishing schooner (Industry) near White Head, who gave him information that several American schooners were at anchor at Two Island harbor, and that they got their wood and water at White Head. They fired several muskets on their anchoring, and told the crew of the Industry they would not allow a man-of-war's boat to board them, and after they completed their wood and water they shifted to Two Island harbor. We got the yawl under weigh about nine o'clock in the evening, and went towards Two Island harbor, and anchored about two o'clock in the morning. At daylight we observed several vessels at anchor at Two Island harbor and shortly after got under weigh, when we chased them; observed three of them lashed together, and all the crews collected on board the middle one. We ordered them to separate, which at first they refused to do, until Mr. Jones threatened to fire on them; they dropped clear of each other. We boarded them and detained the American schooners Reindeer and Ruby. Mr. Jones asked the master of the other two American shallops if they were willing to take the crews of the Reindeer and Ruby on board for a passage home; they answered they were willing to do so. Mr. Jones gave them as much provisions as they chose to take and put them on board, with the exception of the masters. About eight o'clock we made sail, Mr. Jones in the Reindeer and myself in the Ruby, for St. Andrews. While beating up through East Quaddy, about six p. m. when abreast of the Harbor de Lute, observed two schooners coming down towards us full of armed men and wearing American colors, one of them making towards me and the other to Mr. Jones. The one abreast of me ran alongside and boarded with about forty-five men with pistols, swords and muskets, and fixed bayonets. When they got on board they took possession of the Ruby and took the arms from my crew. One of the men with his musket and fixed bayonet made a thrust at one of my men named James Lloyd (marine) but Mr. Howard, leader of their party, parried the thrust off. The man again attempted to knock the marine down with the but-end of his musket, which Mr. Howard again parried off and ordered him not to use violence against any of my men. As he had got possession of the vessel, and which was all they wanted, they then fired off all their muskets and pistols which were loaded. I observed the other schooner fire off muskets likewise. Then I asked for the arms of my crew, which they gave me; we then shoved off and left them. After we had left and rejoined the yawl, they fired several volleys of musketry on board both schooners all the way to Eastport.

Q. What quantity of wood and water had the Ruby on board?

A. There were two casks with water on deck, but cannot say whether there was any below, nor can I say what quantity of wood there was on board.

Q. How was the wind?

A. A moderate breeze from the north-west.

Q. How was the weather?

A. Fine clear weather till we had possession of the schooners, and then it came on foggy and cleared off again in the afternoon.

Thomas Richardson, seaman, examined.

Question. Were you in the yawl with Mr. Jones when he detained the American schooners Reindeer and Ruby?

Answer. Yes.

Q. Relate what you know respecting their detention.

A. I remember going in the small boat with Mr. Jones; after pulling some time we launched the boat over a bar about half a mile broad, between two islands, and afterwards we boarded an English fishing schooner. The crew informed us that the schooners at anchor off Two Island harbor were American fishing vessels, and had the night before fired two guns and defied any man-of-wars' boat boarding them, and advised us not to attempt to board them in the small boat we were then in; we then returned to Gull cove that night with the whole of the crew in the yawl, and pulled during the whole of that night, and at day break we were within three miles from four schooners at anchor a little more than a mile from the shore; we observed them get under weigh, and three of them lashed alongside each other. Mr. Jones then desired them to separate, which they did not do for some time, when Mr. Jones threatened to fire on them; they then separated and dropped astern of each other and anchored. We then boarded them and took possession of the Reindeer and Ruby, and the crews, as I understood with their own consent, went on board of two other vessels. We then got the Reindeer and Ruby under weigh and made sail for St. Andrews; when in East Quaddy two schooners came towards us, fired a gun and hoisted American colors; observed one of the schooners take possession of the Ruby, and the other came close to us and desired us to heave to. I was at the helm when they fired at us, and the shot came close to me and Mr. Jones; there was but one musket on board of us, which Payne, a marine, wanted to fire, but Mr. Jones desired him not; I observed the American schooner's deck full of armed men with muskets, pistols and carbines. After they had fired at us Mr. Jones gave up the papers to the master of the Reindeer who held them up in his hand to the Americans and desired them not to fire, as he had possession of the vessel. We then went in the yawl for St. Andrews; some of the Americans would insist on taking the yawl with them; I observed them fire volleys of muskets till after they had anchored the Reindeer and Ruby at Eastport.

Q. How was the weather when Mr. Jones detained the Reindeer and Ruby?

A. It was clear weather till after they were detained, then it became foggy.

Q. Do you know what quantity of wood and water the Reindeer had on board?

A. The quantity I cannot recollect, but we used from both.

JAMES LLOYD, marine, examined.

Q. Were you in the yawl with Mr. Jones when he detained the American schooners Reindeer and Ruby.

A. Yes.

Q. Relate the particulars respecting the detention.

A. I remember a man at Gull cove giving information of some schooners, (American,) the particulars I do not know. We got under weigh that evening in the yawl and pulled all night; after daylight we got close to four schooners, and observed three of them lashed alongside of each other, and the crews of these vessels on board the larger one. Mr. Jones ordered them to separate several times, and at length he said he would fire into them; they were very abusive to us; after a considerable time they separated, and we boarded them. Mr. Jones then sent me below to see if there were any fire-arms on board the Reindeer; I found a musket with a double charge and primed, and two powder horns full of powder, and about twelve or fourteen pistol balls. Mr. Jones obtained two of them with the consent of the master of the other two vessels and the crew of the two detained. They were allowed to go on board, and take what provisions they pleased; the masters of the vessels came on board and took green fish, pork, tea, butter, molasses, flour and bread. I was sent with Mr. Towneau on board one of them, and got under weigh in company of the one Mr. Jones was on board of, and in the afternoon of the same day, while beating up to St. Andrews abreast of Campo Bello, I observed three schooners and two boats; one of the schooners went towards Mr. Jones and fired several muskets; went below to get my dinner, when Mr. Towneau called us up to our arms, and asked me if my musket was loaded. I told him it was and primed; he told me he thought they were American armed vessels coming to take us; I then asked Mr. Towneau if I should fire, he said not until he gave me the orders. They came nearly alongside us, and ordered us to heave to; they presented their muskets with fixed bayonets at us, and said—damn your eyes, if you don't heave to, we will fire into you. They sung out to the man at the helm if he did not put the helm down and lower the peak they would shoot them dead on the spot. They then came alongside and boarded us; I think about forty men in number, all with muskets and fixed bayonets except one, for our deck was full of armed men. They told me to deliver up my arms or they would run me through; damn your eyes, said one; and another said I will blow your brains out. I replied, I am a king's man and will not deliver up my arms; their leader drew his sword and had a brace of pistols; desired the Americans not to trust any of us. At that time a man made a thrust at me with fixed bayonet which their leader parried off; the same man again made a blow at me with the but-end of his musket, which their leader again parried off; then their leader told me that I had better give up my arms and he would be answerable for them, which I did; about this time they fired volleys of musketry.

We then went on board of our boat, and observed them continue to fire as they were returning to Eastport.

Q. What kind of weather was it when Mr. Jones detained the Reindeer and Ruby?

A. Fine weather with a light breeze, but came foggy after.

Q. Do you know what quantity of wood and water was in the schooner you were on board of?

A. Two casks and a half of water and about a cord of wood.

JOHN CAMISH, seaman, examined:

Question. Were you in the yawl with Mr. Jones when he detained the American schooners Reindeer and Ruby?

Answer. I was.

Q. Relate the particulars.

A. I recollect Mr. Jones going out from Gull cove in the small boat and returning the same evening. I heard him say that he had information of some American schooners. We were ordered to get our things in the yawl from the tent, and went out that evening. We pulled the greater part of the night and anchored for about an hour and a half. At daylight observed five vessels lying at anchor; when they saw us they got under weigh, when we came near them, one of the vessels dropped her anchor and two others lashed alongside her, and the crews of these vessels went on board the centre one with their fish spears. Mr. Jones desired them to separate, which they did not do for a considerable time, until Mr. Jones threatened several times to fire into them; they separated and we boarded the Reindeer, where I remained. Mr. Jones detained her and another vessel. By the wish of the crew of these vessels and by the consent of the masters of the other two vessels, they were put on board with as much provisions as they wished. The masters of the two vessels not detained came on board us in their own boats and took the crews with as much provision as they chose on board. We then got under weigh the Reindeer for St. Andrews, the Ruby in company. In the afternoon of the same day observed two armed vessels; one of them came towards us, gave three cheers, and hoisted American colors; they called to us to heave to, and threatened to fire into us. Her decks were full of armed men with muskets and fixed bayonets. There was also in company a large armed boat. The schooner fired two musket balls across our decks, and then Mr. Jones gave up the papers to the master of the Reindeer, who held them up in his hand and called to the Americans not to fire, as he had possession of the vessel. The American schooner was then about half pistol shot from us. We were then ordered into the yawl by Mr. Jones and observed them, in going to Eastport, fire volleys of musketry.

Q. What quantity of wood and water had the Reindeer?

A. Three barrels of water and a great deal of wood.

Q. What weather was it when the vessels were detained?

A. Fine weather and light winds from north and west.

RICHARD NEWLAND, seaman, examined.

Question. Were you in the yawl with Mr. Jones when he detained the American schooners Reindeer and Ruby?

A. Yes, I was.

Q. Relate the particulars.

A. I recollect a man coming to Mr. Jones at the tent at Gull cove, and informing him that some American fishing schooners had come into an anchorage not far from us, and fired their muskets, and said they would not allow any man-of-war's boat to board them; they got their wood and water there, and got under weigh and ran to Two Island habor, laid there one day and at night. I was left on shore in the tent, and remember Mr. Jones going out in a small boat, with four hands, and returned the same afternoon. We got under weigh that evening in the yawl, and stood for Two Island harbor. The next morning we fell in with four American schooners and two English. When I first saw them they were at anchor about half a mile from the land, in Two Island harbor. After they saw us, they got under weigh. On our chasing them we fired to bring them to, but instead of complying three of them run alongside each other and lashed together. When we came close to them Mr. Jones desired them to separate and bring up. They refused to do so, and would not allow us to board, until Mr. Jones repeatedly threatened to fire into them; they dropped clear of each other. We then boarded the Reindeer, and Mr. Jones asked what they were doing there. They said they came in to land their gurry and offal of the fish, and get wood and water. Mr. Jones told them they had time enough to get their wood and water at White Head. Mr. Jones detained the Reindeer, and then boarded the Ruby, which vessel he detained also; and I was sent below in the Ruby to search for arms; found none; but found a frying pan full of hot lead and a spoon in it, and some musket balls quite warm. I asked the master of the Ruby where his arms were. He said he had none, except a fowling-piece. I then asked him where it was. His reply was, he could not say, unless his boy had lost it, or stowed it away in the salt-room. When I asked their reason for lashing together, and running the musket balls, they said they intended to keep us off with their five-and-thirty men and eight muskets; they would have easily done so. I then asked them where their eight muskets were. They answered they had eight muskets. The masters of the two schooners which were not detained came on board the Ruby, and took her crew with their clothes, and as much provisions as they wished for a passage to their home, by their own wish and sanction of Mr. Jones. Afterwards we got under weigh in the Reindeer and Ruby, for St. Andrews, and the same afternoon between Indian island and Campo Bello two schooners came towards us full of armed men. The one abreast of the Ruby gave three cheers, and hoisted American colors, bore down and ordered us to heave to, which we refused doing, till they threatened to fire into us. They came alongside and boarded, with muskets and fixed bayonets, cutlasses and pistols. I do not know the number of men, but our decks were full. They took our arms from us and discharged their own. We then were ordered into our boat, and I observed them firing volleys of musketry going in, and after they had anchored at Eastport.

Q. Did you search the salt-room of the Ruby for arms?

A. No, I had not time.

Q. How was the weather when the Reindeer and Ruby were detained?

A. Fine clear weather with a little breeze, but came on foggy afterwards for two hours.

A. How was the wind?

A. I cannot recollect.

William Vickery, marine, examined:

Question. Were you in the yawl with Mr. Jones when he detained the American schooners Reindeer and Ruby?

A. Yes.

Q. Relate all the particulars you know respecting their detention?

A. I recollect going out in the small boat from Gull cove with Mr. Jones, and after pulling for a short time we launched the boat over a bar between two islands and boarded an English fishing schooner; the crew informed us that two American schooners had anchored the night before not far from where we laid, and that they fired their muskets and defied any man-of-war's boat to board them. The crew of the English schooner told us that we had better be well armed, as the Americans were prepared for us; we returned to Gull cove and in the evening went out with all the crew in the yawl; we pulled till about four o'clock in the morning; at daylight observed some schooners at anchor which vessels shortly after got under weigh, and as we went down towards them I fired by the direction of Mr. Jones to bring them to; as we closed the vessels, three of them lashed alongside each other, and put their crews on board the middle one. Mr. Jones desired them to cast off from each other, which they refused to do for some time, till he threatened to fire into them, when they separated and we boarded the Reindeer, and Lloyd, a marine, was sent down to search for arms; he found one musket loaded. Mr. Jones asked the master where the arms were that he saw; he said he had none. Mr. Jones then detained the Reindeer and Ruby, and by the wish of the crews of these vessels, with the exception of the masters, they were put on board the other two Americans not detained, with consent of the masters, taking with them as much provisions as they chose. We then got under weigh in the Reindeer, with the Ruby in company. In the afternoon of the same day when abreast of Campo Bello I saw two schooners, one of which came towards us, fired a gun and hoisted American colors and ordered us to heave to, which we refused to do, and after we tacked they fired across our deck; after this Mr. Jones delivered up the papers to the master of the Reindeer, who held them up to the Americans and desired them not to fire. We were then ordered by Mr. Jones into the yawl, and I observed them fire several muskets at a time and the balls falling into the water as they were going into Eastport.

Q. What arms had the Americans?

A. I observed some men with cross belts, bright muskets and fixed bayonets, others with muskets, swords and pistols.

Q. What quantity of wood and water had the Reindeer on board?

A. A cask full below, some on deck, and plenty of wood.

Q. How was the weather when the Reindeer and Ruby were detained?

A. Fine weather with fine breezes.

Q. How was the wind?

A. I do not recollect.

Q. Did you search the salt-room on board the Reindeer for arms?

A. No, I did not.

JOHN LLOYD, seaman, examined:

Question. Were you in the yawl with Mr. Jones when he detained the American schooners Reindeer and Ruby?

Answer. Yes.

Q. Relate the particulars.

A. I went out with Mr. Jones from Gull cove in a small boat, and after pulling for some time, we launched the boat over a bar about a quarter of a mile broad, between two islands, and boarded an English schooner, (Industry, of Grand Manan,) and I heard the master inform Mr. Jones that some American fishing schooners had been in there on the last Saturday and discharged three guns, and that several were now lying in a bay further on, when Mr. Jones proposed to go after them in the small boat; but the master of the Industry advised not to do so, as they were well manned. We returned to Gull cove the same day, and in the evening went out with all the arms in the yawl, and at daylight next morning observed five schooners getting under weigh. We ran down to them and fired. Observed three of them made fast to each other; the largest of them in the middle, with the crews collected on board of her. Mr. Jones ordered them to separate, which they hesitated to do for some time, and they appeared to be consulting together. After Mr. Jones threatened to fire into them they separated. We boarded two of them, the Reindeer and Ruby, and the crews of these vessels, with the exception of the masters, went on board the two schooners not detained, with as much provisions as they pleased. After this we got under weigh in the Ruby and Reindeer in company for St. Andrews. On the afternoon of the same day, when abreast of harbor De Lute, observed two schooners coming down from Eastport full of men. One of them came towards us, and all hands hailing us to heave to or they would fire into us; they ran alongside and boarded us, with about thirty or forty men, with muskets and bayonets. As they were shearing up alongside, some of them sang out to fire at the officers, and fire at the man at the helm. They had their muskets levelled at us, when their leader (a young man) came among them and said, "don't fire at all," and parried their muskets off. They took our arms from us and drove us forward. I saw a scuffle between James Lloyd, a marine, and one of the Americans who wanted to take his arms from him. Mr. Towneau told us to get into our boat; and I observed them firing volleys of musketry and cheering on their way to Eastport. Also observed firing on shore at Eastport.

Q. What quantity of wood and water had the Ruby on board when detained?

A. Two or three casks, with plenty of wood.

Q. How was the weather?

A. Very fine, with light breezes.

William Payne, marine, examined:

Question. Were you in the yawl with Mr. Jones when he detained the American schooners Reindeer and Ruby?

Answer. Yes, I was.

Q. Relate all the particulars respecting her detention.

A. I recollect one Sunday going out from Gull cove with Mr. Jones in the small boat, and after pulling for some time hauled the boat over a bar; shortly after boarded an English fishing schooner belonging to Grand Manan. The crew gave us information that some American schooners anchored there on Saturday night, fired their guns and said that they did not care for any man-of-war's boat whatever, as they were as well armed as the men-of-war's boats. I saw the schooners at Two-Island harbor at anchor when on board the Industry, and her crew said we had better not go to them in the small boat, that it was their determination to kill us. We then returned to Gull cove, and in the evening of the same day got under weigh in the yawl with all the crew and proceeded to Two-Island harbor. About daylight next morning observed them get under weigh; we chased them and fired to bring them to. I then saw them closing together, and three of them lashed alongside each other; we ordered them to separate, which they seemed not willing to do. Mr. Jones threatened to fire into them; we had our muskets (two in number) pointed to the vessel; after being threatened several times Mr. Jones asked two of them, the Reindeer and Ruby, what brought them there; their answer was that they came for wood and water. Mr. Jones then said, when you had got it what was your reason for not going away; their reply was, the breeze was so light they could not get out. The crews of their vessels, with the exception of the masters, by their own request went on board the two schooners not detained, and were allowed to take what quantity of provisions they thought proper. I then went below with Thomas Richardson to search for arms by the direction of Mr. Jones; found a loaded musket in the cabin. Mr. Jones asked the master what become of their arms; he said they were below; we then went again below for the same purpose. Mr. Jones again asked the master of the Reindeer what became of the arms; his answer was that they must have been hove overboard; he said, we had got them yesterday killing ducks. Shortly after we got the Reindeer and Ruby under weigh, and proceeded for St. Andrew's in the afternoon of the same day. When abreast of Campo Bello saw a schooner coming down and run close alongside the Ruby; hoisted American colors; observed another standing towards us in the Reindeer; they gave three cheers, hoisted American colors and hailed us to drop the peak of the main-sail. The master of the Reindeer said to us you had better not fire on them, as they will kill every man of you, and he ran below. They came near us and Mr. Jones said, come alongside us, which they were willing to do. I had my musket ready to fire and asked Mr. Jones if I should do so; to which he objected, and said let them come alongside first; they then fired and a ball passed close to us. Mr. Jones gave the papers up to the master of the Reindeer, who held them up to those on board the American schooner, desired them not to fire, and said that we would quit the vessel as soon as possible. We then got into the yawl and observed them firing different times going into Eastport.

Q. When the schooner with American colors flying came close, did you observe the crew armed?

A. Yes, they were, and her deck full of men armed with muskets and fixed bayonets, carbines, blunderbusses, pistols and swords.

Q. How was the weather when the Reindeer and the Ruby were detained?

A. Fine weather and a fine breeze.

Q. What quantity of wood and water had the Reindeer on board?

A. Two casks of water on deck, and plenty of wood.

Q. Did you search the salt-room and the hold for arms?

A. No; I did not search the salt-room aft, but did forward.

JOHN CHASE, seaman, examined:

Question. Were you with Mr. Jones in the yawl when he detained the American schooners Reindeer and Ruby?

Answer. No, I was not; I was one of his boat's crew, but was left behind at St. Andrews.

We, the undersigned, have examined the aforesaid persons belonging to her Majesty's sloop Dotterel, taking the minutes of these depositions respecting the detention of the American fishing schooners Reindeer and Ruby; and we do declare that their evidence has been taken in a very impartial manner, and that the persons aforesaid have not been biassed in any way whatever.

JOHN COOK, *Senior Lieutenant.*
JAMES HAZZARD, *Purser.*
RICHARD HOARE,
Commander of her Majesty's Sloop Dotterel.

Evidence of Mr. Towneau, midshipman, and the crew of the yawl-boat belonging to his Majesty's sloop Dotterel, relative to the detention of the American schooner Rebecca.

Mr. TOWNEAU, midshipman, examined:

Question. Were you in the yawl when Mr. Jones detained the American schooner Rebecca?

Answer. Yes.

Q. Do you know Mr. Jones's reason for detaining her?

A. Mr. Jones went down to board an English schooner, and one of the men who was on board, by the name of Wright, as pilot, belonging to an American schooner, told Mr. Jones that his vessel came in for wood and water; at which Mr. Jones appeared to be satisfied, and on leaving the schooner saw the American schooner getting under weigh; ran down and fired several shots across her bows to bring her to; she not heaving to, chased her across the Bay of Fundy. About eight p. m. of the same day lost sight of her. Some days afterwards observed the same schooner at anchor near Gull cove, cleaning fish and heaving the gurry overboard. Mr. Jones detained her, and she was subsequently taken to St. John's.

Q. How was the weather?
A. Perfectly clear and fine weather, with a moderate breeze.
Q. Was it fair wind to the fishing ground?
A. Yes; we sailed in that direction.

—

THOMAS RICHARDSON, examined:

Question. Do you remember the circumstances relative to the detention of the American schooner Rebecca?

Answer. Yes.

Q. Relate all you know about her.

A. When we first intended to board her she made sail from us; we then chased her over to the Nova Scotia shore, where we lost sight of her about eleven p. m. About three or four days after we again saw her at the Grand Manan, lying about a mile from the shore, cleaning fish, throwing the garry overboard. Mr. Jones then detained her and carried her to St. John's.

Q. Where was she lying?
A. In some harbor at the Manan, but cannot recollect the name.
Q. What quantity of wood and water do you think she had on board?
A. About three or four forty-gallon casks, and about two cords of wood.
Q. How was the weather when you boarded her?
A. Fine weather and clear, with a moderate breeze.
Q. Do you know whether the wind was fair for the fishing grounds?
A. Yes; the wind was fair.

—

FELIX SHAW, private marine, examined:

Question. Were you in the yawl with Mr. Jones when he detained the American schooner Rebecca?

Answer. Yes.

Q. Relate what you know about her.

A. She came to anchor with another schooner in a small harbor in the Grand Manan. While we were lying there the foretop-sail schooner got under weigh, and we boarded her; while on board of her the other weighed and made sail. We then made sail after her, and chased her across the Bay of Fundy over to the Nova Scotia shore, where we lost her after dark. Some days after we saw her again at anchor within a mile of the shore, near Gull cove, throwing the garry overboard. Mr. Jones seized her and took her to St. John's.

Q. What quantity of wood and water had she on board?
A. I do not recollect.
Q. How was the weather when you detained her?
A. The weather was fine and clear, with a light breeze.
Q. Was the wind fair for the fishing ground?
A. I do not know the position of the fishing ground.

JAMES LLOYD, private marine, examined:

Question. Were you in the yawl with Mr. Jones when he seized the American schooner Rebecca?

Answer. Yes; I was.

Q. Relate what you know about the detention of her.

A. While lying at anchor in the harbor, I believe the Grand Manan, I saw the schooner come in and anchor. While Mr. Jones was boarding another vessel under English colors, observed the master and two men go off to the schooner and immediately get under weigh; when they got around the point of land lost sight of her.

Q. Where were you when you lost sight of her?

A. On shore, cooking the boat's crew's provisions.

Q. How do you know it was the master who went on board the vessel?

A. The people at the store told me so; and said he had been there frequently and had asked them for water, which they had refused him. His reply was, if he could not have it by fair play, he would be damned if he would not have it by foul.

Q. When did you again see the schooner?

A. I never saw her again.

Q. When did you rejoin the yawl?

A. Next morning.

Q. Do you remember the schooner Rebecca being detained?

A. I was put on board a vessel and with the rest of the crew carried her to St. Johns; I believe her name was Rebecca, but am not certain.

Q. Do you remember when this vessel was detained?

A. I do not exactly recollect, but believe it to be a week or more after rejoining the yawl.

Q. What quantity of wood and water had she on board?

A. I believe there was half a hogshead three parts full, and a considerable quantity of wood.

Q. How was the weather?

A. Quite fine and clear with moderate breezes.

Q. Do you know the position of the fishing ground?

A. I do not.

JOHN CAMMISH, seaman, examined.

Q. Were you in the yawl when Mr. Jones detained the American schooner Rebecca?

A. Yes.

Q. Relate all you know about her.

A. The first time I saw her she was at anchor in a small harbor in the Grand Menan, and when we made after her she got under weigh and we chased her, keeping her in sight till about eleven p. m., when we lost sight of her on the Nova Scotia shore.

Q. Did you see her again afterwards?

A. Yes, about three days afterwards.

Q. Relate where she was then and what she was doing?

A. She was lying in a small harbor about four or five miles from Gull cove, cleaning her fish.

Q. What quantity of wood and water had she on board?
A. She had plenty of both when we detained her.
Q. Do you know the quantity in casks?
A. Two and a half hogsheads.
Q. How was the weather when you boarded her?
A. Fine weather with a little breeze.
Q. Do you know how the wind was?
A. I am not positive but believe it was from the northwest.

RICHARD NEWLAND, seaman, examined:

Question. Were you in the yawl when Mr. Jones seized the American schooner Rebecca?

A. Yes, I was.

Q. Relate the circumstances.

A. She came in and anchored while we were lying in the Grand Menan; when going to board her she got under weigh and made sail; we chased her across the Bay of Fundy over to the Nova Scotia shore, when we lost sight of her about 11 p. m. Three days after we again saw her at anchor near Beal's passage cleaning her fish and heaving the gurry overboard; we boarded her and took her to Gull cove.

Q. What distance was she from the land when she was taken possession of?

A. About a quarter of a mile.

Q. Did you hear Mr. Jones ask what they were doing there?

A. Yes, and said they came in for water.

Q. What quantity of wood and water had they on board?

A. About two barrels and a half of water and about a cord or a cord and a half of wood.

Q. How was the weather when you boarded her?

A. Fine clear weather with little breezes.

Q. Do you remember if it was a fair wind for the fishing ground?

A. Yes, it was.

WILLIAM VICKERY, marine, examined:

Question. Were you in the yawl when Mr. Jones seized the American schooner Rebecca?

Answer. Yes, I was.

Q. Relate what you remember respecting her.

A. On boarding an English schooner at or near Gull cove, we saw another lying there; while going on board observed another getting under weigh and made sail; we chased her across the Bay of Fundy and lost sight of her between nine and ten o'clock p. m.

Q. When did you again see the schooner?

A. About three or four days after at anchor within Gull cove, within half a mile of the land, cleaning fish. Mr. Jones boarded her and took possession of her.

Q. Did Mr. Jones ask what they were doing there?

A. Yes, he did, and they said they came for wood and water.

Q. What quantity of wood and water had they on board?

A. I believe about a barrel and a half of water and about a cord and a half of wood.

Q. How did you know it was the Rebecca?

A. I was informed by one of the crew that it was the same vessel which we chased across the bay and that they would have hove to, but did not know we were in chase of them, and that the captain said, had he not returned, but made the best of his way home, he should not have been taken.

Q. Did you fire at her to bring her to?

A. Yes, I was ordered by Mr. Jones to fire across her bows, and I fired seven times.

Q. How was the weather when you detained her?

A. Fair weather with a nice breeze.

Q. Do you know if it was a fair wind to the fishing ground?

A. No, I do not.

JOHN LLOYD, seaman, examined:

Question. Were you in the yawl with Mr. Jones when he seized the American schooner Rebecca?

Answer. Yes, I was.

Q. Relate what you know of the circumstances.

A. When lying in Gull Cove I heard two or three men, who I believe were fishermen belonging to the island of Grand Menan, say that the schooner we had chased across the Bay of Fundy two or three days before, was then at anchor between two islands about a mile and a half round the point. We boarded her and detained her. She was then cleaning fish.

Q. Did you hear Mr. Jones ask what they were doing there?

A. Yes, they said that they came in for wood, water, and to land their gurry.

Q. What quantity of wood and water had they on board?

A. They had as much wood as would last them for a fortnight, and had a full cask of water on deck and some below, but cannot say how much, besides beer.

Q. How was the weather when you detained her?

A. It was fine weather with a moderate breeze.

JOHN CHEESE, seaman, examined:

Question. Were you in the yawl when Mr. Jones detained the American schooner Rebecca?

Answer. Yes, I was.

Q. Relate what you recollect relative to the detention of her.

A. We were lying alongside a wharf in a harbor in the Menan, and observed two schooners at anchor under the land. We went out and boarded an English schooner, on board of which was a man belonging to the Rebecca, acting as pilot while on board the schooner; got under weigh and ran across the Bay of Fundy. We gave chase to her and fired several shot across her bows to bring her to. At about half past ten p. m. lost sight of her. On the fourth day afterwards we again fell in with her at anchor in a narrow passage in the Menan; boarded her and found them cleaning their fish and throwing the gurry overboard. Mr. Jones asked what they were doing there; they said they had come in for wood and water.

Q. What quantity of wood and water had they on board?

A. Two quarter casks full on deck and some in the hold, but don't know the quantity, and had about a cord and a half of wood.

Q. How was the weather when you detained her?

A. Fine weather and a light breeze.

Q. Do you know if the wind was fair for going to the fishing ground?

A. Yes, it was.

We, the undersigned, have examined the aforesaid persons, belonging to his Britannic Majesty's sloop Dotterel, taking the minutes of their depositions respecting the detention of the American fishing schooner Rebecca, and we do declare that their evidence has been taken in a very impartial manner, and the persons aforesaid have not been biassed in any way whatever.

JOHN COOKE,
Senior Lieutenant of his Majesty's sloop Dotterel.
JAMES HAZZARD, *Purser.*
RICHARD HOARE, *Commander.*

Mr. Brent to Mr. Vaughan.

DEPARTMENT OF STATE,
Washington, February 2, 1826.

SIR: I have the honor to refer you to a letter which was written by Mr. Adams to Mr. Stratford Canning on the eve of his departure from this country, (the 25th of June, 1823,) enclosing copies of a complaint and protest which had been just received at this department, in reference to the capture and detention of a fishing vessel belonging to George Moody, of York, in the State of Maine, by a British gun-brig, called the Argus, and soliciting the good offices of that gentleman, in the first instance, to obtain the restitution of the vessel to Mr. Moody, and in the next, to claim indemnity and reparation due to him and others for the capture and interruption of the vessel in question; and likewise to Mr. Canning's letter in reply, under date the 1st July following, which states that he would take an early opportunity of referring the papers to the proper authorities for the purpose of inquiry and attaining the ends of justice.

To satisfy the inquiries of Mr. Moody as to the result of Mr. Canning's reference of his case, will you have the goodness, sir, to inform me whether that result is known to you, or, if it be not, to take the necessary steps for procuring a decision upon the case, and to communicate that decision to this department.

I pray you, sir, to accept the assurances of my distinguished consideration.

DANIEL BRENT.

The Right Hon. CHARLES R. VAUGHAN,
Envoy Extraordinary and Minister Plenipotentiary from Great Britain.

Mr. Vaughan to Mr. Clay.

WASHINGTON, *February* 5, 1826.

SIR: I have the honor to acknowledge the receipt of your note, dated the 2d inst., calling upon me to enable you to satisfy the inquiries of Mr. Moody about the result of the reference of his case to the British government, by my predecessor, Mr. Canning, complaining of the capture of a fishing schooner, his property.

Upon a reference to the archives of this mission, I find that the complaint of Mr. Moody was referred, in the first instance, to the rear admiral commanding the British naval force at Halifax, and that, subsequently, in a despatch dated November 15, 1823, a communication from the British admiralty was transmitted to Mr. Addington, his Majesty's chargé d'affaires at Washington, informing him that the schooner Charles had been regularly condemned in the vice-admiralty court of the Province of New Brunswick, and that it was not expected that the government of the United States would lend further countenance to the complaints of the owner.

The condemnation of this vessel took place upon the grounds of a breach of the act of the 59th George III, chap. 28, for the protection of the British fisheries, and which act was passed in conformity with the stipulations of the convention concluded between his Britannic Majesty and the United States, on the 20th October, 1818.

The circumstances attending this capture are detailed in a note addressed by Mr. Addington, his Britannic Majesty's chargé d'affaires, to the minister of the United States having the Department of State, dated the 12th of October, 1823. I have the honor to refer you to that despatch, which contains the documents in explanation of this capture received from the rear admiral upon the Halifax station, and to request you to accept the assurances of my highest consideration.

CHAS. R. VAUGHAN.

Mr. Vaughan to Mr. Clay.

WASHINGTON, *April* 29, 1826.

SIR: On the 5th October, 1824, Mr. Addington, his Majesty's chargé d'affaires, addressed a note to the government of the United States, in which he stated that an outrage had been committed by some armed citizens of the State of Maine, in forcibly rescuing, off Eastport, two American vessels, the Reindeer and Ruby, which had been captured by his Majesty's cruisers while fishing in the Bay of Fundy, in places where the United States had by treaty renounced the right so to do.

No answer having been given by the government of the United States to the remonstrance made by Mr. Addington, I am directed to ask for an acknowledgment of the impropriety of the conduct of the persons concerned in the forcible recapture of the above mentioned vessels.

In all complaints which the government of the United States has had occasion to bring forward against his Majesty's cruisers employed in the protection of the British fisheries in the Bay of Fundy, the fullest investigation into every case of alleged misconduct has been instituted by the

British agents, and the reports of the commanding officers have been laid before the American government. If it has been necessary to call for the judgment of the colonial tribunals, prompt and impartial justice has been administered, in proof of which I have only to refer you to the case of the American ship Charles, which had been legally detained, but having been illegally employed by her captors after her detention, was restored.

I ask with confidence, on the part of his Majesty's government, for an acknowledgment of the improper conduct of the persons engaged in the forcible recapture of the Reindeer and Ruby, as the British government is disposed to waive all demand for the punishment of the offenders, as the act resulted apparently from unpremeditated violence.

I request that you will accept the assurances of my highest consideration.

CHAS. R. VAUGHAN.

Mr. Bankhead to Mr. Forsyth.

WASHINGTON, *January* 6, 1836.

The undersigned, his Britannic Majesty's chargé d'affaires, has the honor to transmit to the Secretary of State of the United States the copy of a letter which he has received from the Earl of Gosford, his Majesty's governor-in-chief of Canada, enclosing letters from the officers of the customs at Quebec and Gaspé, in which serious complaints are preferred against fishermen of the United States, for encroaching on the limits of the British fisheries carried on in the river and gulf of St. Lawrence.

These encroachments have occasioned great injury to the British merchants and others engaged in connection with these pursuits, and moreover, they are entirely at variance with the restrictions imposed by the convention which was concluded in the year 1818, for regulating the fisheries carried on by the two nations.

The undersigned begs leave to call Mr. Forsyth's attention to the repeated acts of irregularity committed by the fishermen of the United States, detailed in the letter from the sub-collector of customs of Gaspé, and he confidently hopes that measures will be taken to prevent their recurrence, and do away with the possibility of collision taking place on the spot, which might arise should those fishermen persist in encroaching upon forbidden ground.

The undersigned avails himself of this opportunity to renew to Mr. Forsyth the assurance of his most distinguished consideration.

CHARLES BANKHEAD.

The Hon. JOHN FORSYTH, &c., &c., &c.

Lord Gosford to Mr. Bankhead.

CASTLE OF ST. LEWIS,
Quebec, *December* 26, 1835.

SIR: Having received complaints of encroachments by the fishermen of the United States, on the limits of the British fisheries carried on in the river and gulf of St. Lawrence, and of the injury thereby occasioned to the merchants and others engaged in that pursuit, I conceive it to be my duty to transmit for your information the enclosed copies of communications made to me by the officers of the customs here and at Gaspé upon this subject.

I beg leave, at the same time, to observe that I have forwarded similar copies to his Majesty's vice admiral, commanding on this station.

I have the honor, &c.,

GOSFORD.

CHARLES BANKHEAD, Esq., &c., &c., &c.

The sub-collector of customs at Gaspé to the collector and comptroller at Quebec.

CUSTOM HOUSE, *Gaspé, September* 12, 1835.

GENTLEMEN: I beg leave to acquaint you that for several years past numerous complaints have been made by those who carry on the fisheries on the shores of the river and gulf of the St. Lawrence, against American fishermen who frequent the fishing banks, for having from time to time encroached their limits, to the serious injury and prejudice of the British merchants or "planters," who have much capital involved in that precarious pursuit.

The circumstance of immense numbers of United States fishing smacks forming a line and ranging themselves on the banks where the codfish chiefly resort, has been often referred to as a principal cause why the fisheries have visibly retrograded, inasmuch as the *waste* is thrown overboard in the process of curing, deterring the fish from seeking food at their former summer resorts; but as the convention made in 1818, and ratified by the statute 59 George III., chapter 38, secures to the republican government of the United States certain privileges and limits, our merchants have suffered the obstruction without complaint.

The United States fishermen have not, however, remained content with the great indulgences afforded them by the treaty, but, under numerous pretexts, approach our shores in direct violation of its restrictions; and, for several years past, have had the temerity to take bait even on our beaches. But in order to elucidate and convey some idea in what manner their infringements can so materially affect the success of our fishermen, it may be desirable to explain, in brief terms, the nature of the process itself, as practised here.

At the commencement of the fishing, early in May, an abundant supply of caflin and herring are obtained for bait, and when the influx of these ceases, mackerel make their appearance, and our fishermen, by putting out nets and moorings have, until lately, been amply supplied with that fish as a substitute to bait their hooks. But the United States fishermen having adopted a new system of mackerel fishing, by feeding them under their vessels, (large schooners of one hundred tons, and frequently fifteen to twenty men) not only take immense quantities, but by their proximity to the shores entertain the fish from being taken in the nets; and it has now become a universal practice with them to intrude wherever they please, without reference to any given law or restriction; and I have detected, with various success, several of their vessels under such circumstances.

On a recent voyage in the custom-house boat, down the bay of Gaspé, I met three large schooners fishing for mackerel between the shores and the fishing barges, not two miles from land, and remonstrated with the master of one (the Bethel, of Provincetown.) They were all in the act of fishing, and although I advised the said master to go off, he declined doing so, offering nothing in vindication but scurrilous contempt, and my means were inadequate to enforce any measures of redress.

As each succeeding year renders the foregoing evils more manifest, coupled with reiterated complaints by the merchants engaged in the trade here, and carrying on fishing, I have considered it my duty respectfully to draw your attention to the case, begging, in behalf of our enterprising settlers, that you will be pleased to lay the same before vice admiral the commander-in-chief, at Halifax.

For several years after my appointment to this survey, we were favored with at least annual visits of his Majesty's cruizers, and particularly during the commands of Admirals Griffith and Sir Charles Ogle, and a knowledge of this presence or vicinity was a salutary and efficient protection to the Gaspé fisheries, but for some time past scarce any ship of war has called here.

It is unnecessary to remark that the harbor of Gaspé, a harbor which may rank almost first in his Majesty's dominions, affords safe and convenient anchorage, easy of access, and capable of entertaining any ship of his Majesty's navy; and if the commander-in-chief would be pleased to direct a cruizer to be stationed during the summer months between Point Misco and the entrance of the river St. Lawrence, or so far as the island of Anticosti, including Gaspé bay, our fisheries would be very materially benefited, and a deserving community protected in their pursuits.

In offering the foregoing imperfect detail, I do so as a duty devolving on me in my public capacity, with a hope that I may be excused, and under a conviction that the vice-admiral commander-in-chief, will be pleased to take the case into his high consideration. All of which is most respectfully submitted to him.

I have, &c.,

D. McCONNELL, *Sub-Collector.*

The COLLECTOR AND COMPTROLLER
Of his Majesty's Customs, Quebec.

Collector and Comptroller of Customs to Lord Gosford.

CUSTOMS, QUEBEC, *November* 9, 1835.

MAY IT PLEASE YOUR EXCELLENCY: We have the honor to transmit for your excellency's information, a copy of a letter just received from the sub-collector of this department at Gaspé, with reference to certain complaints made against the United States fishermen for encroachment on the limits and otherwise injuring the British fisheries carried on in the Gulf of St.

Lawrence, in order that your excellency may take such measures therein as the circumstances of the case may appear to your excellency to require.

We have the honor, &c.,

HY. JESSOPP, *Collector.*
CHARLES G. STEWART, *Comptroller.*

His Excellency EARL OF GOSFORD,
Commander-in-chief, &c., &c., &c.

Mr. Forsyth to Mr. Bankhead.

DEPARTMENT OF STATE,
Washington, January 18, 1836.

The undersigned, Secretary of State of the United States, has the honor to acknowledge the note addressed to him on the 6th instant, by Mr. Bankhead, chargé d'affaires of his Britannic Majesty, with its enclosures, complaining of encroachments by the fishermen of the United States on the limits secured, by the convention of 1818, exclusively to British fishermen. Though the complaint thus preferred speaks of these encroachments as having been made from time to time, only one is specifically stated, viz: that of the schooner *Bethel*, of Provincetown. But the President, desirous of avoiding just ground of complaint on the part of the British government, on this subject, and preventing the injury which might result to American fishermen from trespassing on the acknowledged British fishing grounds, has, without waiting for an examination of the general complaint, or into that respecting the *Bethel*, directed the Secretary of the Treasury to instruct the collectors to inform the masters, owners, and others engaged in the fisheries, that complaints have been made, and to enjoin upon those persons a strict observance of the limits assigned for taking, drying, and curing fish by the American fishermen, under the convention of 1818.

The undersigned avails himself of this opportunity to offer to Mr. Bankhead the renewed assurance of his high consideration.

JOHN FORSYTH.

CHARLES BANKHEAD, Esq., &c., &c., &c.

Mr. Bankhead to Mr. Forsyth.

WASHINGTON, *January* 19, 1836.

The undersigned, his Britannic Majesty's chargé d'affaires, has the honor to acknowledge the receipt of Mr. Forsyth's note of yesterday's date.

The undersigned cannot resist expressing to the Secretary of State his high sense of the prompt manner in which the President has been pleased to instruct the collectors of customs to enjoin upon the masters and others engaged in the American fisheries strictly to observe the limits assigned to them by the convention of 1818. It is a new proof of the friendly feeling entertained by the President towards the British government—a feeling fully reciprocated on their part.

The undersigned has the honor to renew to Mr. Forsyth the assurance of his distinguished consideration.

CHARLES BANKHEAD.

The honorable JOHN FORSYTH, &c., &c., &c.

[H. R. No. 186—26th Congress, 1st session.]

VESSELS ENGAGED IN THE FISHERIES SEIZED BY THE BRITISH.

Message from the President of the United States, transmitting a report of the Secretary of State, in relation to vessels of the United States engaged in the fisheries, seized by the British authorities during the year last past.

IN SENATE, *April* 15, 1840.
Referred to the Committee on Foreign Affairs.

To the House of Representatives:

In compliance with the resolution of the House of Representatives of the 23d March last, I transmit a report from the Secretary of State, which, with the documents accompanying it contains the information in possession of the department in relation to the subject of the resolution.

M. VAN BUREN.

WASHINGTON, *April* 10, 1840.

DEPARTMENT OF STATE,
Washington, April 10, 1840.

The Secretary of State, to whom has been referred a resolution of the House of Representatives of the 23d March last, requesting the President to communicate to that house "all the information in his possession, or in the possession of either of the departments, relating to the seizure and condemnation, by the British authorities during the year now last past, of certain American vessels engaged in the fisheries," has the honor to lay before the President copies of all the papers in the Department of State in relation to the subject of the resolution.

JOHN FORSYTH.

The PRESIDENT.

LIST OF PAPERS.

United States consul at Halifax to Mr. Forsyth, 28th of February, 1839.

Same to same, 27th of June, 1839, and enclosures.

Same to same, 8th of August, 1839.

United States consul at Pictou to same, 11th of March, 1839.—Extract.

Same to same, 10th October, 1839.

Same to same, 18th November, 1839, and enclosure.

Same to same, 24th March, 1840.—Extract.

Collector at Frenchman's bay to same, 15th July, 1839.

Mr. Woodbury to the Acting Secretary of State, 1st of August 1839, and enclosures.

First Comptroller to Mr. Woodbury, 17th of June, 1839, and enclosure.

Collector of customs, Boston, to same, 27th of June, 1839, and enclosures.

Acting Secretary of State to the President, 14th of August, 1839.—Report.

Acting Secretary of State to Acting Secretary of the Navy, 9th of August, 1839.

Acting Secretary of the Navy to Acting Secretary of State, 9th of August, 1839.

Acting Secretary of State to Acting Secretary of the Navy, 29th of August, 1839.

Acting Secretary of the Navy to Acting Secretary of State, 30th of August, 1839.

Acting Secretary of the Navy to the Secretary of State, 4th of September, 1839.

Lieutenant Commanding Paine to Mr. Forsyth, 29th of December, 1839.

United States Consul at Halifax to Mr. Forsyth.

[No. 74.] CONSULATE OF THE UNITED STATES OF AMERICA,
Halifax, Nova Scotia, February 28, 1839.

SIR: I have the honor to inform you that the schooners "Hero," of Eastport, Harvey, master, and "Combine," of Boston, Kennison, master, have been seized and condemned in the court of vice-admiralty for an alleged violation of the several treaties on the subject of the fisheries. The decree for condemnation passed the 28th of January, but no sale has taken place.

The case of the "Hero" was not brought before my notice, but the owner and master of the "Combine" applied to me, as consul; but the case was clear against the vessel, upon her master's own admissions, taken upon oath. And as the seizure was made at the Gut of Canso, which Mr. Primrose claims to be within his jurisdiction, alleging that his commission is "for the port of Pictou, and for all other ports and places that may be nearer to Pictou than the residence of any other consul," under these circumstances, I declined putting in any defence, acquainting the owner with my determination, which had been formed after submitting the case to counsel.

I have the honor to be, sir, your obedient, humble servant,

JNO. MORROW.

Hon. JOHN FORSYTH,
Secretary of State, Washington.

United States Consul at Halifax to Mr. Forsyth.

[No. 77.] CONSULATE OF THE UNITED STATES OF AMERICA,
Halifax, Nova Scotia, June 27, 1839.

SIR: I have to state that a number of American vessels have been seized in this Province for violating, as has been alleged, the convention between the United States and Great Britain, and the law of this Province, a copy of which I forwarded in my letters numbered 41 and 63, namely:

Schooner Shetland, of Boston, 98 tons burden, seized at Whitehead, near Canso.

Schooner Magnolia, of Vinalhaven, seized at Tusket Island harbor, near Yarmouth.

Schooner Independence, of Vinalhaven, seized at Tusket Island harbor.

Schooner Hart, of Deer Isle.

Schooner Java, of Islesborough.

Schooner Charles, of Mount Desert, seized at Canso; this vessel has been released.

Also, a schooner, name unknown, seized at Guysborough.

Schooner Mayflower, of Boothbay, seized and sent into Guysborough.

Schooners Battelle, Hyder Ally, and Eliza, seized at Beaver harbor.

I enclose copies of two letters, which I thought it my duty to write to the Governor, with several statements submitted to him. Also, a copy of an affidavit, made by the master and crew of the schooner Eliza, of Portland; and a copy of a letter addressed to me by Sir Rupert D. George, baronet, Secretary of the Province; also, a report made by the Queen's advocate general in the matters referred to the Governor.

You will perceive, from the papers now transmitted, the position in which I am placed: urging the claims of the owners and masters of the vessels, and having the expense of the crews to pay, they being utterly destitute; and I have been compelled to afford them the assistance they required.

I have received information that the revenue-cutter Hamilton had arrived at Yarmouth, for the purpose of inquiring into the circumstances of those seizures, and I wished most earnestly to have seen her commander; but it is now said that she has proceeded to St. John's, N. B. And although I have felt the impropriety of my interference in the business of the consulates of St. John's, N. B., Pictou and Sidney, (Yarmouth and the Tuskets being nearer to St. John's than to Halifax—Whitehead and Guysborough being nearer either to Sydney or Pictou,) I could not refuse my assistance to American citizens in distress; and I hope this will pass without censure.

I beg leave, also, to refer to the Journals of the House of Assembly, now transmitted, from which it would appear that the provincial act has been principally framed on the documents therein contained.

Many other vessels will no doubt be seized, and I shall be called upon by the crews of the vessels to intercede for them, and to supply their wants. This I took the liberty of bringing under your notice in my letter No. 62; and I respectfully urge that the labor of protecting the interests of American citizens in this province should not, of necessity, devolve on me, as living near the seat of government, while all the perquisites of office are enjoyed by others within whose consular jurisdiction the seizures have been made.

I have the honor to be, sir, your obedient, humble servant,

JOHN MORROW.

The Hon. JOHN FORSYTH,
Secretary of State, Washington.

[Enclosures in the preceding.]

REPORT.

I have carefully examined the foregoing letter and statements made by Mr. Morrow, the American consul, to his excellency, and submitted to me by his excellency's order, and most respectfully report thereon: That it does not appear to me that his excellency can be called upon, in the case referred to, to interfere and stay proceedings in the court of vice-admiralty, which alone has jurisdiction over the subject-matter. Several of the cases alluded to were commenced during my absence from home; and the evidence in these cases has not yet been submitted to me.

In the cases of the vessels at Yarmouth, commissions have been issued to examine witnesses, which are not yet returned.

The three American schooners seized at Beaver harbor, by Mr. Darby, have been proceeded against by me as advocate general, and the examination duly taken; whereby it appears that the crews of two of them had actually fished with set nets in that harbor, and had taken fish on board therefrom the night before the seizure; and this evidence is confirmed by the mate of one of those vessels, an American subject. In the case of the third, which is one of those noticed by Mr. Morrow, the evidence at present is not so conclusive. In the case of the seizure by Mr. Forrester (alluded to) the evidence has not been submitted to me; but I will call for it, as in the other cases, before any other proceeding is had, after the return of the monition.

In all cases where the evidence is not complete on the part of the seizers, no decree will be urged by default against vessels or cargo, until the most ample time and opportunity are afforded the owners or others concerned to make defence, which I shall feel it my duty to allow them to do in such cases upon the most favorable terms which by law can be granted. And in any case where there does not appear good cause of detention and prosecution, I will exercise my own discretion, as in the case referred to in No. 1, now enclosed; which course, I hope, will meet the approbation of his excellency and her Majesty's government.

S. G. W. ARCHIBALD,
Advocate General.

June 20, 1839.

CONSULATE OF THE UNITED STATES OF AMERICA,
Halifax, Nova Scotia, June 15, 1839.

SIR: In the interview with which your excellency honored me a few days ago, I took the liberty of expressing my opinion with respect to the recent seizure of several American vessels, in the ports of this Province, by Mr. Darby and Mr. Forrester.

I now beg leave to solicit the attention of your excellency to a statement of facts, so far as they have come to my knowledge, and to bring them plainly before your excellency. I have abstracted from affidavits now in my possession, and which, if necessary, may be submitted to your excellency, all that I think may enable your excellency to form a correct judgment on the cases respectively; which papers are hereunto annexed, and numbered 1 to 6.

I would state to your excellency that Mr. Matthew Forrester declared to me, on the morning of Saturday last, in the presence of several respectable persons, that he gave money to the boy referred to in statement No. 1, (the case of the Shetland,) to induce the master to sell the articles named in that statement; and, in mentioning this circumstance, I am unwilling to imagine that your excellency will sanction a practice by which individuals, and especially strangers and foreigners, may be entrapped at the instance of officers appointed to carry the laws of the country into effect, and who are interested in the condemnation of property so placed in jeopardy.

I would earnestly request your excellency to consider the cases which I now place before your excellency, and which, I think, do not, under all the circumstances, subject the vessels to forfeiture under the provisions of the convention between Great Britain and the United States.

With respect to the operation of the provincial act, William IV., cap. 8,

I would only respectfully refer your excellency to the act itself. I do not presume to express an opinion regarding it; but would only notice the utter impossibility of any defence being offered by a master of these small fishing vessels, even if conscious of his innocence.

In the tenth section of the act it is said, "that no person shall be admitted to enter a claim to anything seized in pursuance of this act, &c., until sufficient security shall be given, &c., in a penalty not exceeding sixty pounds," &c.

Your excellency will please to observe that, under this rule, a claimant must be in a situation to procure funds to employ lawyers, and to pay heavy court expenses under the vice-admiralty table of fees; which cannot be done in any of these cases, as I am informed by professional men, under an advance of at least thirty or forty pounds currency; adding to this the security of sixty pounds, it is evident that the owner of each vessel so seized must either send on funds or letters of credit to the extent of one hundred pounds, before he can oppose the seizure, or, otherwise, the vessel will or may be condemned by default.

This sum is, perhaps, as much as any of these small vessels are worth, and the claimant, if able to pay it, must actually place at hazard the one hundred pounds mentioned, in addition to his property seized; and although, perhaps, quite innocent of any offence, must depend upon the proverbial uncertainty of litigation for the recovery of any part of the property or money in such danger.

I would also respectfully urge that I dare not plead for those persons who have actually offended; but, as the organ of certain individuals who may have erred in a slight degree, either from ignorance or from temptation, and violated the provisions of an act of which they may never have heard, I beg, if it be possible, that your excellency will interfere for their relief; and, if it is consistent with truth and justice, to exercise the high powers with which you are invested; and, perhaps, under the advice of her Majesty's council, your excellency may be enabled to extend mercy to such as have not wittingly offended.

In any case in which an apparent and wilful infringement of the convention or of the law has been made, I have no wish to interfere.

I have the honor to be, sir, your excellency's humble servant,

JOHN MORROW.

His Excellency Lieut. Gen. Sir Colin Campbell, *K. C. B.*,
Lieutenant Governor and Commander-in-chief, &c.

A true copy: JOHN MORROW.

Consulate of the United States of America,
Halifax, Nova Scotia, June 18, 1839.

Sir: I have received from Guysborough letters of which I beg leave to annex copies of two, and an extract from one; and I respectfully request that your excellency will be pleased to consider the cases thus submitted.

In addressing your excellency, I am constrained to remark, that the port of Guysborough is out of my district, and the case in question should properly have come under the notice of Mr. Primrose, at Pictou, or Mr. D'Wolfe, at Sydney; but, if the statements made to me are to be relied on, I feel it to be my duty, independent of form, to beg that your excellency will be pleasd to wave a matter of form, and permit me to urge the claims of a poor, and I think injured man.

In doing so, however, I wish to disclaim any interference with the consulates at Pictou or Sydney; but it would appear that the cargo of the vessel seized at Guysborough will perish, and the crew must be ruined, unless prompt measures are adopted for their relief.

If the statements are correct, I am not aware that an officer of the provincial government has a right to inquire whether a vessel of the United Sates sails under a mackerel or a codfish license. Something I know is necessary to establish the national character of the vessel; but if herring instead of codfish or mackerel are taken, provided those herrings are taken in comformity with the convention, I have most respectfully to urge that Mr. Marshall could not possess a right to seize a vessel under such circumstances, even if the master had erred in fishing at the Magdalen Islands; and that Mr. Marshall is only clothed by your excellency with authority to protect the interests of this province, while the Magdalen Islands, where the offence, if any, has been committed, belongs to the province of Lower Canada.

I have copied the letter from the master of the schooner Charles verbatim, that no mistake or misapprehension may attach to me.

I have the honor to be, sir, your excellency's humble servant,

JOHN MORROW.

His Ex'cy Lieut. Gen. Sir Colin Campbell, *K. C. B.*,
Lieutenant Governor and Commander-in-chief.

A true copy: JOHN MORROW.

No. 1.

Schooner Shetland, of Boston, Massachusetts, G. W. Clare, master, burden 98 tons.

This vessel sailed from Boston, on the 20th day of May last, on a fishing voyage to the Labrador coast, victualled and stored for about three months; having no object in view save the procuring of a cargo of fish, not intending to trade, nor having any goods on board for sale when the vessel left Boston, but having a few suits of oil clothing, intended for the crew, as is usual.

After leaving Boston, encountered a succession of easterly winds, and after having been driven about for some time, put into the harbor of Whitehead on the 3d of June, for shelter, and to obtain wood, but were informed that no wood could be had, except soft wood; the mate and two hands then collected a small quantity of wood lying on the shore. At 2 p. m., before the mate went on shore, the schooner drifted, and the small bower chain, of which about thirty fathoms were out, parted about fifteen fathoms from the anchor; let go the best bower anchor, and narrowly escaped being driven on shore. [The declaration of the mate to me, not in the affidavit referred to, is, that the vessel was about her own length from the rocks.] Then carried out the kedge anchor, by way of a second anchor, with a hawser and a coil of large rigging attached to it. At about 4 p. m. recovered the anchor and part of the chain. About 6 a. m. on the following day, got under weigh, and came to in American cove, in Whitehead harbor, to procure wood and place the vessel in safety. That a lad, whose name is unknown, came on board the schooner. [Supposed to be about sixteen years of age. This not in the affidavit.] Requested the master to sell him a pair of trousers, which he (the master) refused to do, but on repeated importunities consented that the young man might select a pair; the boy also requested to have some tea and tobacco, and, after much hesitation, the master, having none to spare, and not having either beam, scales, or weights on board, gave him a quantity of tea, supposed to be about one pound, and about six to eight pounds of tobacco; for which articles, namely, the trousers, tea, and tobacco, the boy paid to the master four dollars. About two hours after this transaction, a number of men came on board, headed by a person who was said to be a magistrate or custom-house officer, and demanded the papers of the schooner, (the register, fishing license, and the log-book,) which he retained; sent the master and the crew on shore at Whitehead, except the mate; the vessel was then seized, and has been brought to Halifax. It has since been ascertained that the schooner was seized by Mr. Matthew Forrester.

List of articles shipped on board of said schooner at Boston, as nearly as can be ascertained.

Beef about 1 barrel; pork do.; tea 28 pounds; tobacco 20 pounds; bread $\frac{3}{4}$ barrel; flour $1\frac{1}{2}$ do.; meal 3 bushels; rice 20 pounds; chocolate 1 box; gin about 30 gallons; oil skin suits 6; fishing gear 1 seine; [this is called seine—I believe it is a large net,] salt about 36 hhds. in barrels; coffee 25 lbs.; molasses $1\frac{1}{8}$ barrel; butter 25 lbs.; potatoes, turnips, and onions, small quantities; empty barrels 305; brooms 1 dozen; oil 3 gallons; candles 10 lbs.; and a box containing tinware, essences, &c., value $25, intended for Monsieur Chevalier Revier, Bon Esperance, Labrador.

What quantity of articles remain on board is not exactly known. They neither caught, nor were preparing to take fish on the coast. Were in no harbor from the time of leaving Boston until the said vessel was seized, and had not bought or sold any articles on the coast, save the trousers, tea, and tobacco before mentioned.

A true copy: JOHN MORROW.

No. 2.

Case of the schooner Magnolia, of Vinalhaven, State of Maine. George Pool, master.

Affidavit of George Pool, master, William S. Coombe, David Joice, and Samuel Clarke, seamen.

Left Vinalhaven the 26th April last on a fishing voyage into the Bay of Fundy.

Fished at the distance of forty miles, and never at a less distance than fifteen miles from the coast of Nova Scotia, until about the end of April.

In want of water.

Blowing very heavy.

Followed an English vessel into Tusket Island harbor.
Remained there about twenty hours.
Neither the master nor any of the crew of the schooner took or caught ny herring, cod, or other description of fish, within fifteen miles of the oast.
Master admits that he purchased a barrel of herring for bait, but took o fish within fifteen miles of the coast of Nova Scotia.
Remained, as before mentioned, at Tusket island, and returned to the ishing ground at not less than fifteen miles from the coast, and there reained until the 25th day of May.
In want of wood and water.
Blowing a gale of wind from the southeast. Returned to the Tusket slands on Saturday, the 25th day of May, having on board forty quintals f fish.
On Sunday, the 26th day of May, the vessel seized by Mr. Darby, and aken into Yarmouth.

A true copy: JOHN MORROW.

No. 3.

Case of the schooner Independence, of Vinalhaven, State of Maine, 31 tons.

At Vinalhaven about the 10th of April last; fitted for a fishing voyage into the Bay of Fundy.
Sailed on or about the 10th of April; commenced fishing, but never at a less distance than fifteen miles from the coast of Nova Scotia, until the latter end of April last.
In want of water; went into the Tusket Islands, and remained at anchor about twenty hours. At the expiration of that period put to sea, and returned to the fishing-places in the said bay; but not fishing at a less distance from the coast than fifteen miles.
Remained in the bay until the 25th day of May. The only compass on board the vessel having been broken, the master wished to reach Yarmouth to have his compass repaired, and to obtain a supply of water. Blowing a gale of wind, the weather thick and hazy, was compelled to take shelter in Tusket Islands for the night.
On the 26th May, lying at anchor, the schooner was boarded and seized by Mr. Darby, commanding the schooner Victory, who demanded all the papers of the said schooner, which were delivered to him.
The vessel taken into Yarmouth; crew ordered to leave the vessel.
Protest made in the usual form.

A true copy: JOHN MORROW.

No. 4.

Case of the schooner Hart, J. Turner master, from Deer Island, State of Maine.

Deposition of the master, and Hiram Rich and Albert Douglas, Americans residing at Yarmouth, and Robert Power, seaman.

Sailed from Deer Island on a fishing voyage in the Bay of Fundy, and remained there at a distance not at any time less than fifteen miles, until the 30th May last.

Except when compelled by stress of weather, or the want of necessary fuel and water, to put into harbor, and for no other purpose, put into Tusket Islands, and once into the port of Yarmouth.

The master never, at any one time, remained in any harbor or place for a longer period than twenty-four hours; that neither he nor his crew, since her departure from Deer Island, have taken or prepared to take fish of any kind or description with nets, lines, or in any manner, at a distance from the coast less than fifteen miles.

That the said master went into Tusket harbor to procure wood and water, and for no other purpose whatever.

That Benjamin Brown, a resident at Yarmouth, while lying in harbor, called to one of the crew of said vessel, requesting that the said master would assist him in clearing or picking his nets; and —— ——, of the boat Hart, in consequence of such request, went on board of Brown's vessel, (a British vessel,) and assisted in clearing his nets; for which service Brown gave to the deponent Rich about two barrels of fresh herrings.

[The master and crew state that they had no need of bait, having abundance of clams on board, which had been brought with them from Deer Island. This, however, not in the affidavit made at Yarmouth.]

That, with the exception of the two barrels of fish, neither the master of the said boat, nor her crew, have fished on any part of the coast of Nova Scotia within fifteen or sixteen miles.

That no article whatever has been sold from or out of the said vessel; but the necessary supply of wood and water were obtained and paid for in money.

That, on the 21st day of May, the boat was boarded and seized by Mr. Darby, of the government schooner Victory, and taken into Yarmouth, and all the papers of the said schooner Hart were taken from the said master, and himself and crew were sent on shore; Mr. Darby detaining all the clothes and necessaries of the said master and crew, except the clothes they had on at the time of seizure.

The affidavit of Benjamin Brown, of Yarmouth, Nova Scotia, taken before —— Parish, Esq.

[This affidavit came to my hands on Wednesday, the 11th June, by mail.—J. M.]

That he, Brown, had been engaged in the herring-fishery at the Tusket Islands since 17th of April.

That about the 1st day of May last, the American boat Hart was seized by the commander of the schooner Victory.

That the said boat Hart came to the said island frequently, when, in his belief, shelter was necessary. The boat was always brought to anchor close to deponent's vessel; and verily believes that no herring or other kinds of fish were taken by the crew of said boat within or near to the said islands.

Saith, that when said boat entered the said islands, had her crew attempted to fish or to set nets deponent must have been aware of it, as the said boat always came to anchor close to deponent's vessel.

Deponent saith, that about four weeks since he gave to the master of the said boat, and to one of her crew, named Rich, two and a half barrels of herring, as a recompense for assisting him, (deponent,) at his request, in picking herrings from deponent's nets, and in dressing and salting his fish.

A true copy:

JOHN MORROW.

No. 5.

Case of the schooner Java, of Islesborough, State of Maine.

This case has not been reported at the consulate, but a claim has been made for the passage of four seamen to the United States.

A true copy:

JOHN MORROW.

No. 6.

PROVINCE OF NOVA SCOTIA, *Halifax, ss.*

Personally, on this 13th day of June, A. D. 1839, before me, John Morrow, consul of the United States of America for the port of Halifax, in the Province of Nova Scotia, and for all other ports and places that may be nearer to Halifax than the residence of any other consul, came and appeared James Morton, master of the schooner "Eliza, of Portland," which is of the burden of fifty-eight tons or thereabouts, together with the several parties whose names are hereunto subscribed, being the crew of the said schooner, who, being by me duly examined and sworn on the Holy Evangelists of Almighty God, did testify and declare to be true the several matters hereinafter set forth:

That, on or about the twenty-sixth day of April last, these appearers sailed in and with the said schooner from Portland, on an intended fishing voyage on the coast of Nova Scotia and the Bay of St. Lawrence, having on board materials and stores fit and proper for a fishing voyage, and which voyage was expected to last about four months.

That the said schooner carried no articles whatever suitable for a trading voyage or for sale; nor had any one of these appearers any goods, wares, or merchandise wherewith to carry on any trade or traffic, but solely intended and fitted out for the fishery, with nets, hooks and lines, salt, &c.

That from the day on which they sailed, they never caught or cured any fish whatever, within ten or twelve miles of any part of the coast; and never made any harbor, except when unavoidably compelled to do so, viz: on or about the 5th of May, it blowing a heavy gale from the east, they were compelled to make a harbor in the Ragged Islands, where they remained two or three days, during all which period the weather continued so bad as to prevent their going to sea. On the 24th of May, or thereabouts, the schooner having carried away one of her larboard main-chains, in consequence of a heavy swell while at anchor in sixty fathoms off Spry harbor, they were compelled to run into Beavet harbor as the nearest port, and got it repaired by a man whose name they were informed was ——— Winsell.

That on the 8th of June now instant, the said schooner put again into Beaver harbor to get wood and water, (their supply being much reduced, and being inadequate for the said voyage,) and on the 9th (being Sunday) the said schooner was seized by the provincial schooner Victory, Darby master, and brought to Halifax; the master and the cook being the only persons allowed to stay in her.

And these appearers solemnly declare that they neither sold, bartered, nor parted with any article whatever out of the said schooner, or caught or procured or prepared, or intended to catch or procure any fish whatever, except at a distance of ten to twelve miles from the coast of Nova Scotia; or purchased or endeavored to purchase any fish of any of the inhabitants or others on the British coasts, and that the whole sum of money in possession or control of this appearer, the master, did not exceed four to five dollars, or thereabouts, with which to buy wood and water in case of need.

JAMES MORTON,
BENJAMIN MORTON,
his
LEWIS × HAZEL,
mark.
ROBERT MORTON,
JAMES W. GRAY,
SAMUEL BURNS.

Sworn to at Halifax, this 13th day of June, A. D. 1839, before me,
[L. S.] FREDERICK LE BLANC,
Notary Public.

A true copy: JOHN MORROW.

PROVINCIAL SECRETARY'S OFFICE,
Halifax, June 25, 1839.

SIR: Your letter of the 15th instant, and the several papers which accompanied it, relative to the seizure of certain American fishing vessels, having been referred, by the direction of the Lieutenant Governor, to her Majesty's attorney general, I have it in command from his excellency to transmit to you the enclosed copy of that officer's report, and to state that, under the circumstances therein mentioned, his excellency does not consider it proper to interfere in any of the cases which you have felt it your duty to bring under his excellency's notice.

I have the satisfaction to acquaint you, with reference to your communication of the 18th instant, that, before it was received, the attorney general had sent instructions to Mr. Marshall, the seizing officer at Guysborough, for the release of the schooner Charles.

I have the honor to be, sir, your most obedient servant,

RUPERT D. GEORGE.

JOHN MORROW, Esq.

A true copy:

JOHN MORROW.

United States Consul at Halifax to Mr. Forsyth.

[No. 78.] CONSULATE OF THE UNITED STATES OF AMERICA.
Halifax, N. S., August 8, 1839.

SIR: Since I had the honor to address you, under date the 27th June, (No. 77,) several proceedings have been had with respect to the vessels therein named; some have been released on payment of expenses, and others have been condemned.

I beg leave, most respectfully, to recapitulate the fate of each vessel:

The schooner Eliza, of Portland, has been released on payment of expenses, amounting in all, to £84 17*s.* 10*d.*, (this currency,) or $339 56; this, however, contains my commission on cash advanced to release her, and incidental charges connected with a bottomry.

Schooner Shetland, of Boston, released in a like manner; her expenses about $600; but the money was paid by a house of business here, and I do not know the exact amount.

Schooner Charles discharged without any expense.

Schooner Mayflower, of Boothbay, released; her expenses amounted to £75 6*s.* 4*d.*, which I paid. Incidental charges included in this sum.

The Eliza, Charles, and Mayflower have evidently been brought under the operation of a law which I cannot but feel is exceedingly severe—perhaps I should say unjust. It was thought advisable, however, to pay the sums at which they were assessed, rather than have the vessels detained, and, perhaps, subjected to further difficulty.

The Shetland stood in a different position, and escaped condemnation by the merest accident.

The Battelle and Hyder Ally have been condemned and sold.

I bought the former for the owner, who has come on to this place and claimed her. I charged him five per cent. commission, which he paid. He took a sea-letter for Boston from this office, the schooner's papers being filed in the registry of the court of vice-admirality.

The Magnolia, Independence, Java and Hart were condemned in the court of vice-admirality on the 5th instant; and an order has gone to Yarmouth for the sale to take place immediately.

The owner of the two former is here, and he will proceed to Yarmouth to purchase them.

I have a power of attorney from the owner of the Hart to purchase for him; and I have given directions that the Java may also be bought on account of the owners, if it be possible, by so doing, to save these poor men from ruin.

The Hyder Ally remains in my possession, and will, I think, be claimed in a few days, as the owner has written respecting her.

A new case has arisen: The schooner Amazon was seized by the collector of light duties, at the Gut of Canso, and the master transmitted an affidavit to me relating the circumstances of the seizure. I immediately applied to the advocate general, who, after a few days, handed me an order for her release, addressed to the seizing officer, but left open, so that I might send it to the person having the vessel in custody, it being reported that the collector of light duties had absconded.

The master of this vessel will have to pay the expenses attendant on his detention and custody, for which I have become answerable; and how I am to be reimbursed I do not know.

I have the honor to be, sir, your obedient, humble servant,

JOHN MORROW.

Hon. JOHN FORSYTH,
Secretary of State, Washington.

[Extracts.]

United States Consul at Pictou to Mr. Forsyth.

"CONSULATE OF THE UNITED STATES,
"*Pictou, March* 11, 1839.

"SIR: I have to acknowledge the receipt of your letters of the 1st January and 2d February; the latter granting me leave of absence until the 1st of April. But as the season is now so far advanced, I have determined to postpone my intended journey for the present.

"You have, no doubt, been informed by the consul at Halifax of the seizure of several fishing vessels of the United States on the coasts of this Province during the past year, for alleged infringement of the convention of 1818; one of which vessels at least, if not more than one, has recently been condemned in the court of vice-admiralty at Halifax.

"Numerous complaints have been made by the inhabitants of the Province, alleging that the fishermen of the United States frequently violate the terms of that treaty, by following the fish too close to the coasts of Nova Scotia and Prince Edward's Island, and using the harbors thereof for other purposes than are enumerated in the convention.

"The British government has decided to send out two armed vessels in the spring, to be stationed during the fishing season on these coasts, for the purpose of preventing any infringements of the treaty; and although I am well aware that *much* of the outcry which has been made on this subject has had its origin in the disappointed feelings of Nova Scotia fishermen, on seeing themselves so far outstripped in the successful pursuits of so valuable a branch of commerce, by superior perseverance and skill of their enterprising neighbors, yet I know that, within my consular district, a tempting shoal of fish is sometimes, either from ignorance or the excitement of the moment, followed across the prescribed limits; and I suppose that during the ensuing season the greatest vigilance will be displayed in looking after offenders.

"I have thought it my duty to communicate these facts to you, in case it should be deemed requisite, in order to prevent fishermen from becoming unconsciously liable to confiscation; that some instructions should be issued to collectors of customs likely to grant licenses to fishermen, directing them to request the fishermen to make themselves well acquainted with the terms of the treaty, as they may expect a strict enforcement of its provisions during the ensuing season, or to enable you to provide such other remedy as the case seems to demand.

"The Hon. JOHN FORSYTH,
"*Secretary of State, Washington.*"

United States Consul at Pictou to Mr. Forsyth.

[No. 13.]

CONSULATE OF THE UNITED STATES,
Pictou, N. S., October 10, 1839.

SIR: I beg leave to enclose to you copies of several affidavits relative to difficulties which have been experienced by American citizens during the past season in their intercourse with this Province, and in the prosecution of the fisheries on its coasts; together with copies of the correspondence which I have entered into with the provincial authorities on the subject.

Being in daily expectation of a definite reply to my communications to the provincial Secretary, I delayed writing to you, in the hope of being able to lay the whole matter before you at once; but, at the suggestion of Commander Paine, with whom I have recently had an interview, I transmit these documents now, and will forward copies of other communications on the subject as they occur.

The tax of six and two-third cents per ton register of shipping, collected by the Province of Nova Scotia at the Strait of Canso, is levied on British as well as foreign ships; but it becomes a heavy charge on American vessels making four or five trips a year to this port, in the coal trade; and as there is no impost on shipping in American ports for the support of lights on the coast of the United States, such a tax on American vessels in the ports of the British colonies involves a discrepance in the terms of intercourse between the two countries, although it professes to be based on strict reciprocity.

In reference to the affidavits and correspondence, (herewith marked No. 2,) I beg to state that I strictly cautioned Captain Taylor, as well as his crew, to give a fair dispassionate account of the circumstances connected with the detention of the Amazon. The report of the attorney general of Nova Scotia upon this case, to which the letter of the provincial Secretary refers, will, I presume, when received, furnish the defence which may be set up for the conduct of the provincial officer, or point to some means of redress.

I have the honor to be, sir, your most obedient and humble servant,

JAMES PRIMROSE.

The Hon. JOHN FORSYTH,
Secretary of State, Washington.

[Received with Consul Primrose's No. 13.]

No. 1.

CONSULATE OF THE UNITED STATES,
Pictou, Nova Scotia, July 15, 1839.

SIR: I most respectfully beg leave to bring under the notice of the government the existing practice of collecting light-dues at the Strait of Canso.

American vessels bound to Pictou have this season been frequently fired at and brought to at that place, by an armed boat, and boarded by an officer, armed with a cutlass and a brace of pistols, who has enforced payment of light-dues. As but few of these vessels were provided with funds, the masters have been subjected to great inconvenience by being compelled, in many instances, to part with portions of their cargoes or ship's stores, and to pursue other objectionable courses to enable them to meet the demand, which I respectfully submit might be collected here, where the consignees reside, with as much safety to the revenue, and, as you will perceive by the enclosed affidavits, with less danger to strangers, who are led to commit acts seriously affecting the safety of their vessels, through the misrepresentation of an officer claiming to be clothed with authority.

Will you do me the favor of informing me whether the collectors of light-dues at the Strait of Canso act under the authority of the government of this province, in levying that rate there on American vessels not bound to any port or place within the same?

The imposition of any tax by the province of Nova Scotia upon American vessels engaged in the prosecution of the fisheries using that passage *in transitu*, would appear to deprive it of the character of constituting a portion of the high seas.

With the greatest respect, I have the honor to be, sir, your most obedient and humble servant,

JAMES PRIMROSE,
Consul U. S. A.

To the Honorable Sir Rupert D. George,
Provincial Secretary, &c., Halifax.

E. G. Adams, master of the American brig Orleans, of Portsmouth, maketh oath and saith: That on the 10th day of June, now last past, he was at the Gut of Canso, in said vessel, (bound to Pictou for a cargo of coal,) when the Orleans was boarded by Duncan McMillan, collector of light-dues, who demanded payment of light-money. Deponent told said McMillan that he had not a sufficient sum of money on board to pay it; that he was bound to Pictou, where he would get money, and where he expected to pay all his port charges. McMillan, however, insisted on being paid, and told deponent if he had no money he must pay out of the ship's stores; on which deponent, at the request of said McMillan, gave him a barrel of flour, in part payment, having no other means of satisfying the demand.

E. G. ADAMS.

Sworn to at Pictou, the 6th July, 1839, before me,
JAMES PRIMROSE, *Consul U. S. A.*

Nathan Briggs, master of the American schooner Alatamaha, of New Bedford, maketh oath and saith: That on the 19th day of June last past, while said vessel was passing through the Gut of Canso, bound to Pictou for a cargo of coal, Duncan McMillan, collector of light-dues, came on board and demanded to see the Alatamaha's papers, and required payment of light-dues. Deponent said he had no money, but would give an order on Pictou. McMillan looking at the clearance said, "You have no means of paying me on board," and requested deponent to give him a barrel of flour for light-dues. Deponent made answer that he could not break bulk without subjecting himself to a penalty; on which McMillan replied that there was no duty payable on any article delivered to him in payment of light-dues. Deponent believing from the circumstance of a British flag flying in McMillan's boat, that he was an officer of government, and had a right to make such demand, gave him a barrel of flour, and took a receipt therefor, of which the following is a copy, viz:

"*June* 19, 1839.

"Mr. NATHAN BRIGGS, master of the schooner Alatamaha,
"*To the Province of Nova Scotia, Dr.*

"To light-dues for the above vessel, now under your command, for the present voyage from New Bedford, 120 tons.

"Received payment in one barrel of flour.

"DUNCAN McMILLAN,
"*Collector of Light-dues, Gut of Canso.*"

NATHAN BRIGGS.

Sworn to at Pictou, the 6th July, 1839, before me,
JAMES PRIMROSE, *Consul U. S. A.*

HALIFAX, *August* 21, 1839.

Sir Rupert D. George presents his compliments to Mr. Primrose, and regrets not being yet able to reply to his communication relative to the mode of collecting light-dues from American vessels passing through the Gut of Canso. Immediately on its receipt, it was laid before the lieutenant governor and her Majesty's council, and referred to a committee to inquire into the circumstauces; and the committee have not yet made their report.

No. 2.

CONSULATE OF THE UNITED STATES OF AMERICA,
Pictou, August 26, 1839.

SIR: I beg leave to enclose to you copies of two affidavits of the master and crew of the American fishing schooner Amazon, relating to her seizure and detention by an officer of the provincial government at the Strait of Canso.

I most respectfully solicit the favor of being informed of the cause of said seizure; and also, if there has been no sufficient reason for the detention of the Amazon, as would appear by these affidavits, whether the government of the province will be disposed to grant redress to the parties who have thereby sustained such serious and unmerited injury.

I have the honor to be, sir, your most obedient and very humble servant,

JAMES PRIMROSE,
Consul U. S. A.

The Hon. Sir RUPERT D. GEORGE,
Provincial Secretary, &c., &c., Halifax.

Personally came and appeared before me, James Primrose, consul of the United States of America, at Pictou, in the province of Nova Scotia, George W. Taylor, master of the schooner Amazon, of Gloucester, in the State of Massachusetts, in the United States of America; and William Biber, Tobias Nash, James Claney, Edward Claney and John Copeland, all of Gloucester aforesaid, composing the crew of the said vessel; who severally declared that the said vessel having on board fishing stores and supplies, they, the said appearers, set sail in her from Gloucester on the 30th day of June now last past, bound to Labrador, to fish for codfish; that the said vessel arrived at the Gut of Canso on the 4th day of July last, and came to anchor there at Steep Creek cove, for the purpose of procuring wood and water; that, on the next day, said appearers took on board said vessel two barrels of water and two cords of wood; that, thereafter, said vessel remained at anchor there until the morning of Sunday, (the 7th,) on account of the weather being so very foggy that at no time during the said period could appearers discern objects at a distance of thirty or forty yards; that, on the morning of the said 7th, one Duncan McMillan came on board and seized the said vessel, and turned all the said appearers, except the master, on shore in a destitute condition; and the said appearers do severally most solemnly declare that there were no articles on board the said vessel when she left Gloucester aforesaid, but such as are usual and necessary for such voyages; and each appearer, for himself, respectively, declares that no article was sold or delivered from the said vessel, with his individual knowledge or belief, from the time the said vessel sailed from Gloucester aforesaid until she was so seized; nor was any act or thing committed or done by either of the said appearers, respectively, which, to the knowledge of the said appearers, could give any color or pretence for said seizure. And each appearer, for himself, further declares that, during the time which the said vessel remained at anchor at the said Steep Creek cove, as aforesaid, no person whatever warned or requested him to remove the said vessel therefrom.

GEORGE W. TAYLOR,
WILLIAM BIBER,
TOBIAS NASH,
JAMES CLANEY, his x mark.
EDWARD CLANEY, his x mark.
JOHN COPELAND.

Sworn to, at Pictou, Nova Scotia, this 26th day of August, 1839, before me,

JAMES PRIMROSE,
Consul of the United States of America.

Personally came and appeared before me, James Primrose, consul of the United States of America, at Pictou, in the Province of Nova Scotia, George W. Taylor, master of the schooner Amazon, of Gloucester, in the State of Massachusetts, in the said United States, who declared that, in addition to the facts sworn to by him this day, in a joint affidavit with the crew of the schooner Amazon, of Gloucester, relative to the seizure of said vessel at the Gut of Caaso, the following circumstances occurred: That on the arrival of the said vessel at the Gut of Canso, on the fourth day of July last, as stated in the said affidavit, one Duncan McMillan came on board the said vessel, and showed appearer his commission from the government of the province of Nova Scotia as seizing officer and collector of light duties; that the said McMillan demanded from appearer four pence per ton register of said vessel, as light-duty, which appearer paid in silver money, and asked said officer if he could be allowed to take on board wood and water there; to which the said officer replied, that he could take on board as much of both as he wanted, and pay for the wood in goods, if he pleased. It being very foggy, appearer asked if he must leave with his vessel as soon as he got the wood and water on board; to which the said officer replied, that he might stay there as long as he pleased. That the said vessel being detained there by foggy weather for three days, the said officer came on board of her on the morning of Sunday, (the 7th,) and seized her, stating to appearer that he had received information that appearer had landed goods; that the said officer turned the crew of the said vessel on shore, and carried her to Arichat, appearer remaining on board by permission of said officer; that, on their arrival at Arichat, the vessel was hauled into a dock, and the cargo landed, examined and put on board again, with the exception of some articles, which, together with the sails of said vessel, were stored; that the said officer, together with four men, remained on board of said vessel at Arichat for four days, and lived on her provisions, although appearer remonstrated against such conduct; but received for answer from the said officer that the vessel now belonged to him. That said appearer, after endeavoring, unsuccessfully, to get his vessel released at Arichat, proceeded to Halifax, where the United States consul informed him that an order had been sent to McMillan from the government, directing him to release the said vessel; that, on appearer returning to Arichat, he was furnished with the following copy of a letter, said to be addressed to the said McMillan by the attorney general of Nova Scotia:

"Advocate General's Office,
"*Halifax, July* 24, 1839.

"Sir: I have read your account of the seizure of the American schooner Amazon, and the affidavit enclosed; and, although the conduct of the master appears to have been indiscreet, I cannot see any just grounds for her longer detention; and you will therefore not proceed further in this case, but allow the persons who may be entiled to receive the vessel. It must be, however, understood by them, that they cannot continue from day to day in our harbors without a sufficient excuse, which I do not find in this case for the unusual delay which led to the seizure.

"I am, sir, your humble servant,

"S. G. W. ARCHIBALD.

"Mr. McMillan, *Guysborough.*"

That the said McMillian refused to release appearer's vessel unless appearer would discharge a bill presented by said McMillian, of which bill the following is a copy:

Captain Taylor, master of the schooner Amazon,

To Duncan McMillan, Dr.

		£	s.	d.
1839.	To sundry attendance on said vessel - - - - - - - - - - - - - - - -	£21	10	0
	James Turnbull's fees -	1	3	4
	Mr. John Bullam's charges for wharfage, storage, &c.	7	11	1
	Lauchlin McLean's bill for watching vessel - - - - - - - -	3	10	0
		£34	14	5

That appearer being reduced to the alternative of paying the demand, or leaving his vessel in the hands of said McMillan, chose the former, and gave a draft on his owners for the amount; on which his vessel and stores were delivered to him by said McMillan, with the exception of a rifle and a musket, which the said officer took possession of, saying to appearer he thought they would get rusty on board the vessel, and he would take care of them; and they were not returned to appearer, although he demanded them from said McMillan. And the said appearer further declares, that the said vessel was detained in the possession of the said officer from the 7th day of July last, until the 21st day of the present month, being forty-five days, which detention has ruined his voyage, deprived the owner of the power of procuring the bounty for the vessel for this season, and, together with the other heavy expenses incurred by appearer, the whole loss to the owners and crew of the said vessel, in consequence of such seizure, cannot amount to less than from two thousand to two thousand five hundred dollars.

Appearer further declares that he paid five dollars in silver money for the two cords of wood referred to in the joint affidavit of himself and crew, of this date, as taken on board his vessel at Steep Creek cove.

GEORGE W. TAYLOR.

Sworn to at Pictou, this 26th day of August, 1839, before me,

JAMES PRIMROSE,
Consul of the United States of America.

Provincial Secretary's Office,
Halifax, September 3, 1839.

Sir: I have laid before the Lieutenant Governor and her Majesty's Council, your letter of the 26th of August, transmitting copies of two affidavits relating to the seizure and detention of the American fishing vessel Amazon, by Mr. Duncan McMillan; and am directed to acquaint you that copies thereof have been forwarded to McMillan, who is directed to repair to Arichat on Monday next, in order that his conduct on this occasion may undergo a minute investigation before the attorney general, on the receipt of whose report it will become my duty to address you again on the subject.

I have the honor to be, sir, your most obedient servant,

RUPERT D. GEORGE.

James Primrose, Esq.,
Consul United States, Pictou.

No. 3.

CONSULATE OF THE UNITED STATES OF AMERICA,
Pictou, September 28, 1839.

SIR: It becomes my duty to call your attention to the enclosed copy of an affidavit of the master of the American brig Emerald.

The conduct of the collector of light-dues at the Strait of Canso towards vessels of the United States bound to this port, continues to be characterized not only by a total want of courtesy, but very frequently assumes the aspect of open and wanton aggression.

In the hope of receiving your reply to my note of the 15th of July, I have refrained from multiplying complaints; but the nature of the outrage committed on the Emerald requires that I should make the government of this Province acquainted with it.

With great respect, I have the honor to be, sir, your most obedient and humble servant,

JAMES PRIMROSE,
Consul of the United States of America.

Hon. Sir R. D. GEORGE,
Provincial Secretary, &c., Halifax.

Roderick McKenzie, master of the brig Emerald, of Salem, in the State of Massachusetts, in the United States of America, maketh oath and saith: That, on Sunday morning last, the 22d instant, while the said brig was riding at anchor, wind-bound, at the Strait of Canso, on her passage from Boston to Pictou, she was boarded by Duncan McMillan, who demanded to see the ship's papers, which were shown to him by deponent. The said McMillan then demanded from deponent four pence per ton register as light-dues; but deponent informed him that he had not the means of discharging the claim there, but would pay it at Pictou.

McMillan then requested deponent to give him an order on some person at Pictou, which deponent declined to do, saying there was no person there on whom he had any authority to draw. McMillan then left the vessel. About six hours afterwards, when the said vessel was under sail for Pictou, she was boarded by three armed boats, containing about sixteen men, and taken possession of by the said McMillan, but was released on deponent's signing a note-of-hand, payable to the said McMillan or his order on demand, for the amount of the light-duty.

RODERICK McKENZIE.

Sworn to at Pictou, this 24th day of September, 1839, before me,

JAMES PRIMROSE,
Consul of the United States of America.

PROVINCIAL SECRETARY'S OFFICE,
Halifax, September 30, 1839.

SIR: I have the honor to acknowledge the receipt of your letter of the 26th instant, enclosing a copy of an affidavit of the master of the American brig Emerald, relative to the conduct of Mr. Duncan McMillan, collector of light-dues in the Gut of Canso.

Various other complaints against this person having been made to the Lieutenant Governor, the attorney general is directed to inquire minutely into them; and as McMillan may be hourly expected here, I hope to be soon able to reply to the several communications which it has been your duty to address to me on the subject of his alleged misconduct.

I have the honor to be, sir, your most obedient, humble servant,

RUPERT D. GEORGE.

James Primrose, Esq.,
Consul of the United States of America, Pictou.

United States Consul at Pictou to Mr. Forsyth.

[No. 14.]

Consulate of the United States,
Pictou, November 18, 1839.

Sir: I have the honor to acknowledge the receipt of your letter of the 1st ultimo, and to transmit herewith a copy of a letter which I have just received from the Secretary of this province on the subjects which I brought under your notice in my last communication to you, dated the 10th ultimo.

Vessels of the United States trading to this port have paid upwards of $2,800 for "light-dues" during the present year; the aggregate of the tax is greatly increased from the circumstance of its being also collected each voyage from all American fishing vessels (and they are very numerous) using the passage of Canso strait. The claim set up by the province of Nova Scotia, of an exclusive right to the Strait of Canso, is deserving of consideration. If this claim be admitted, the provincial government may at any time impose such restrictions on its navigation as would amount to a prohibition of its use as a commodious access to the fishing grounds in the Gulf of St. Lawrence.

In my letter to you, (No. 11,) dated the 11th March last, I anticipated the difficulties which the fishermen have subsequently experienced upon the coasts of this province. There can be no doubt that some of them were fairly chargeable with infringement of the treaty; I think it equally certain that the excess of zeal displayed by some of the provincial officers in the exercise of their authority, has in certain cases led to unwarranted interference with the rights of the American fishermen, and the liberty of their vessels. I think it is absolutely necessary for their protection that there should in future be at least one small vessel of war commissioned to cruise on the fishing grounds during the summer months, commanded by an active and experienced officer, qualified by prudence and firmness to caution the fishermen against all violation of the treaty, and to guard them vigilantly from every improper molestation.

I have the honor to be, sir, your most obedient and humble servant,

JAMES PRIMROSE, *Consul.*

Hon. John Forsyth,
Secretary of State, Washington.

[With Consul Primrose's No. 14.]

PROVINCIAL SECRETARY'S OFFICE,
Halifax, November 9, 1839.

SIR: The attention of the Lieutenant Governor and her Majesty's Council having been directed, by your letters of the 15th July and 26th September last, to the mode of collecting light-duties from American vessels in the Gut of Canso, that subject has received the best consideration of the board; and I am directed to acquaint you, with reference to the particular cases which you have brought under his Excellency's notice, that the taking of merchandise or ship's stores, instead of money, in payment of light-duty, (as in some few cases appears to have been done,) is, under any circumstances, unauthorized on the part of the collector. The collectors have accordingly been informed that such a proceeding is irregular and unlawful, and must on no account be hereafter resorted to; and it has been further intimated to them, that when the light-duty has been incurred, and its payment after demand has been refused or neglected, the vessel is liable to seizure; but that the law does not give warrant for the use of violence in bringing vessels to in cases where no previous demand has been made; and that the exhibition of fire-arms, while in the performance of their office, is highly reprehensible. The collectors are also instructed not to demand light-duty from vessels bound to Pictou, unless they come to anchor in the strait.

With respect to the concluding paragraph of your letter of the 15th of July, I have it in command to remark that his Excellency cannot admit the character given to the Gut of Canso as a part of the high seas until recognized by some authoritative decision, as the correctness of its application to that narrow passage lying entirely between the lands of this province may be questionable, more especially as an open communication around the eastern end of the island of Cape Breton is to be found on the high seas to the Gulf of St. Lawrence, or any other point to which the Strait of Canso can be made subservient.

I take this opportunity to state that the case of the American schooner Amazon, which was the subject of your letter of the 26th of August, remains under consideration; all the information with respect to it, which is desired, not having been yet obtained.

I have the honor to be, sir, your most obedient, humble servant,

RUPERT D. GEORGE.

JAMES PRIMROSE, Esq.,
American Consul.

[Extract.]

United States Consul at Pictou to Mr. Forsyth.

CONSULATE OF THE UNITED STATES,
Pictou, March 24, 1840.

SIR: * * * I have received no further reply to my application to the Government of this Province, respecting the detention of the Amazon, than that contained in the letter of the provincial Secretary dated the 9th November last.

The (as I apprehend it) unjustifiable detention of that vessel led, not only to the destruction of her intended voyage, but, as I am informed, to her total loss in a gale on the coast of Cape Breton, soon after she was released.

During the past season I heard of several similar causes of complaint as having occurred in my consulate; but as I had not the means of authenticating them, I refrained from making them the subjects of communication to your department.

I feel bound, however, to state as my belief, that, although there may have been good grounds for the condemnation of some vessels, for infringement of the convention of 1818, there has also been, on the part of some of the subordinate officers of the provincial government during the past season, not a little improper interference with the rights of the American fishermen; and, judging from the manner in which the subject has been taken up by the legislature of this Province, now in session, I fear that a repetition of such acts is more likely to be overlooked than reprehended by the provincial authorities.

* * * * * * * *

Collector at Frenchman's Bay to Mr. Forsyth.

District of Frenchman's Bay,
Collector's Office, Ellsworth, July 15, 1839.

Sir: The schooner Charles, Captain Benjamin S. Moore, fitted for the Magdalen Islands herring fishery on the 27th of April last; and after making her fare, on her return put into the harbor called Pirate cove, near the big gut of Canso, and had not lain there twenty-two hours, when the schooner was boarded by an officer of the revenue, called a seizing officer, and by him taken possession of and carried to Guysborough. The only pretence for this seizure was, that the schooner was under codfishing license, and had on board herrings. The vessel, after a detention of nineteen days, was given up by directions from Halifax. That at the time of said seizure, the officer took from him ten barrels of his herrings, which have never been returned; and the remainder of his cargo, by the detention, has been nearly all lost. The name of the seizing officer was John G. Marshall.

Captain Benjamin Moore is a very poor man, and totally unable to bear such a loss. It is at his request I write to solicit the aid of the government in his behalf, knowing of no manner in which he can obtain compensation for his losses from this British officer, but through his own government.

I am, very respectfully, sir, your obedient servant,

EDWARD S. JARVIS.

Hon. John Forsyth,
Secretary of State.

Mr. Woodbury to the acting Secretary of State.

TREASURY DEPARTMENT, *August* 1, 1839.

SIR: I have just received from the State Department a letter addressed to it from Judge Parris, enclosing another from Colonel Thayer, of Lubec, in respect to certain difficulties with the British cruisers and citizens in that neighborhood.

On a perusal of them, I entertain no doubt that it is proper for the State Department to lay those letters before the President for his instructions as to what remonstrance should be made to the British authorities on the subject, and as to the expediency of having a vessel of war visit the coast for the preservation of tranquillity.

This department not appearing to have any power over the matter, the letters are returned, in order that, if deemed proper by you, they may be forwarded to the President.

Respectfully,

LEVI WOODBURY,
Secretary of the Treasury.

A. VAIL, Esq.,
Acting Secretary of State.

[Enclosures in the preceding.]

WASHINGTON, *July* 31, 1839.

SIR: The writer of the letter of which the enclosed is a copy, is a gentleman of high respectability in Maine, whose representations are entitled to entire credit.

At his request, I communicate the facts contained in his letter to the Secretary of State of the United States.

I have the honor to be, sir, with great respect, &c.,

ALBION K. PARRIS.

The SECRETARY OF STATE.

LUBEC, *July* 20, 1839.

SIR: I have this morning been informed that some depredations have already been made upon Grand Menan by our fishing vessels, that now number four or five hundred in the Bay of Fundy, and that a serious attack is in contemplation.

The complaints of the inhabitants of this island have resulted in refusing to our vessels any shelter during bad weather. They are indiscriminately ordered to sea. Three of her Britannic Majesty's armed brigs are cruising in the bay, for the avowed purpose of clearing the coast of our vessels.

Nearly one hundred of our vessels, thus driven from positions secured to them by treaty, are in our harbor and know not what to do. Their licenses are endorsed by the commandants of these British vessels as follows: "Found within the limit prescribed by treaty, and ordered off." One license I saw yesterday endorsed: "Found *fishing* within the limits prescribed by treaty, July 17, 1839.—*J. B. Tarlton, Lieutenant H. B. M. brig Ringdove."

The master of this fishing vessel (schooner Daniel, of Waldoboro') told me that he had been lost in the fog, and used a fishing lead and line to sound with, and that this lead hung over his quarter when boarded.

Towing our vessels indiscriminately to sea, whatever may be the state of the weather, is justified upon the ground that our vessels have no right to enter the Bay of Fundy, much less any of the bays and creeks of the Bay of Fundy.

Our fishermen are generally armed, and will not bear these indignities. They can furnish some thousands of as fearless men as can be found anywhere, at short notice; and, unless our government send an armed vessel here without delay, you will shortly hear of bloodshed: five hundred fishermen, with an average crew of ten men, will not long suffer the tyranny of drunken lieutenants in the British navy.

Please lay this matter before the proper authorities, and oblige your very humble servant,

SOLO. THAYER.

Hon. A. K. Parris,
Second Comptroller, Washington.

First Comptroller to Mr. Woodbury.

Treasury Department,
First Comptroller's Office, June 17, 1839.

Sir: The communication of Messrs. B. and J. M. Leavitt, in reference to the treaty stipulations by which our fishermen are regulated, presenting a question of a diplomatic character, it is respectfully conceived ought to be submitted to the Secretary of State. I therefore return it enclosed.

I am, very respectfully, your obedient servant,

J. N. BARKER, *Comptroller.*

Hon. Levi Woodbury,
Secretary of the Treasury.

[Enclosure in the preceding.]

Boston, *June* 13, 1839.

Sir: Difficulties having occurred in relation to our fishing in the Bay of Chaleurs, Gulf of St. Lawrence, Bay of Fundy, and on the coast of Nova Scotia, we request the favor of instructions as to the fact whether any other, or those treaty stipulations of 1783, are now the regulations by which our fishermen are to be governed.

Very respectfully, your obedient servants,

B. & J. M. LEAVITT.

Hon. Levi Woodbury,
Secretary of the Treasury.

P. S.—We wish an answer for publication to our fishermen, should the department have no objection to our adopting that course.

---

* I may not have the initials of the name correct.

Collector of Boston to Mr. Woodbury.

CUSTOM-HOUSE, BOSTON, *June* 27, 1839.

SIR: The naval officer of this port has, at my request, addressed me a letter on the subject of the late cruise of the Hamilton, in which he bore a part. I enclose a copy of it. I enclose, also, a printed copy of Mr. Grantham's letter.

Captain Sturgis has performed his duty entirely to my satisfaction, and has confirmed the high opinion I had heretofore expressed of him.

Very respectfully,
GEORGE BANCROFT, *Collector.*

Hon. LEVI WOODBURY,
Secretary of the Treasury.

[Enclosures in the preceding.]

NAVAL OFFICE, BOSTON, *June* 27, 1839.

SIR: In reply to your note of yesterday, asking me to state such facts as may have come to my knowledge in relation to the late seizures of American fishing vessels by the British government, I have to say, that during the past week I visited Yarmouth, in the Province of Nova Scotia, and its immediate neighborhood, in company with the officers of the United States revenue-cutter Hamilton, by your permission, with a view to ascertain the names of as many as possible of the American fishing vessels now seized and detained by the British government, with the alleged causes of their seizure and detention. The statement of Henry A. Grantham, esq., our consular agent at Yarmouth, made at my request, and addressed to the commanding officer of the Hamilton, exhibits very fully the facts in relation to the seizure of four of the vessels in question. While at Yarmouth, I had the pleasure of meeting very many highly respectable and intelligent gentlemen of that town, who seemed deeply to regret that their own government officers should have proceeded with so much rigor against the American fishing craft, believing with the consul and the Americans generally, that, in a majority of cases, the seizures had been made for causes of the most trivial character. It is perfectly certain that our fishermen must have the right to resort to the shores of the British provinces for shelter in bad weather, for fuel, and for water, unmolested by British armed cruizers, or this important branch of American industry must be, to a very great extent, abandoned. It affords but poor consolation to the fisherman, whose vessel has been wantonly captured, and who finds himself and his friends on shore among foreigners already sufficiently prejudiced against him, without provisions and without money, to be told that the court of vice-admiralty will see that justice is done him, and that, if innocent, his vessel will be restored to him. The expenses of his defence and the loss of the fishing season are his ruin.

These seizures are made under a colonial law of the province of Nova Scotia. I could not learn what disposition is made of the property seized, after it is decreed forfeited; but I believe it is divided among the persons making the captures. If this be the fact, it will sufficiently explain any discrepancy in the testimony of the witnesses, which may appear in Mr.

Grantham's statement; and it will also, perhaps, explain the eagerness with which these fishing vessels seem to be taken and carried into port for trial.

I learned in Yarmouth, and also on the American coast, in the State of Maine, where our vessel touched for the purpose of landing the two destitute fishermen mentioned by Mr. Grantham, that many more of our vessels had been seized, during the present season, at the Gut of Canso. Some of these seizures have been made for other and different causes from those now detained at Yarmouth. The officers of the British cruisers accuse the masters of these vessels of carrying on an illicit trade in the articles of tea and tobacco with the British subjects of Nova Scotia. I have, from the best authority, the facts in one of these cases: The captain of an American fishing schooner had on board, among other ship's stores, half a keg of tobacco for the use of his crew. An inhabitant of the province came on board his vessel, and, after great importunity, persuaded the American to let him have a few pounds, for which he paid in a small quantity of wood. The purchaser of the tobacco immediately informed the officers of the government; and the vessel, her cargo, and provisions, are now under seizure for this offence. It is, of course, impossible to predict the result of the examination of all the cases in the court of vice-admiralty at Halifax, where they are now pending. The owners and persons interested hope, however, that that tribunal will discriminate between cases of a flagrant and premeditated violation of the treaty and the laws of the provinces, and the mere trivial, unimportant, and fortuitous offences which are described in Mr. Grantham's statement, and which are known to many other persons to have been hastily and very imprudently brought up for adjudication.

In conclusion, permit me to add, that we were received with great courtesy and kindness by the public officers and citizens of Yarmouth; and that we are under special obligations to Mr. Grantham, our consular agent, for the very prompt and obliging manner in which he furnished all the information in his power upon the subject of our inquiry.

I am, very respectfully, your obedient servant,

ISAAC O. BARNES, *Naval officer.*

To George Bancroft, Esq.,
U. S. Collector, &c., Boston.

Consulate of the United States,
Yarmouth, N. S., June 18, 1839.

Sir: At your request, I enclose to you an abridged statement of the depositions of the masters and crews of the four American fishing schooners lately seized by the commander of the British government vessel Victory, and now lying detained in this port; together with a succinct account of my proceedings upon the application to me for assistance by the masters of these vessels.

Upon the 27th day of May last, application was made to me, as the consular agent of the United States at this port, by William Burgess, master of the American fishing schooner "Independence," for advice and assistance, under the following circumstances: On Sunday, the 26th day of May last, while lying at anchor in the Tusket Islands, near the coast of this province, the said schooner was boarded, and, with her cargo and papers, seized and taken possession of by the commander and part of the crew of the British government vessel "Victory," for an alleged infraction, by the crew of the "Independence," of the treaty between Great Britain and the United States, and the laws of this province for the protection of the British fisheries. The schooner was brought into this port stripped of her sails and part of the rigging, and the master and crew obliged to leave her. Depositions of the master, William Burgess, and of the crew, Benjamin Sylvester, Samuel C. Mills, Ezekiel Burgess, and Samuel Burgess, all of Vinalhaven, in the State of Maine, were taken to the above facts, and also to those which follow. They deposed that the schooner Independence, of the burden of thirty-one tons, or thereabouts, and belonging to Vinalhaven, was fitted out and cleared from that port on a fishing voyage into the Bay of Fundy, on the 10th day of April last; and that they continued to fish in the bay (never at any time at a less distance from the coast of Nova Scotia than fifteen miles) until about the last of April of the present year, when being in want of water, and it blowing very heavy, they stood in for the coast, and anchored in the Tusket Islands, where they remained about twenty-four hours.

At the expiration of that time they again put to sea, and remained upon the fishing-ground until the 25th day of May last, when, the compass having been accidentally broken, and there being no other on board, they again stood in for the coast, intending to make the port of Yarmouth, for the purpose of having the compass repaired, and of procuring a supply of water; but the wind being adverse and very violent, and the weather thick and hazy, they were unable to make that port, and were obliged to take shelter in the Tusket islands for the night, at which place they were seized the next day, as before mentioned.

The master and crew of this vessel deposed, most solemnly, that no fish, of any kind or description, had been taken or caught by them during the present season, or since their departure from port, either in the Tusket islands, or at any distance nearer to the coast of Nova Scotia, or of any of the British possessions in America, than fifteen miles; and that at no one time did they remain at anchor in the said islands, or in any port on the coast, for a longer space than twenty-four hours. They however admitted that, at the earnest solicitation of an inhabitant of the Tusket islands, (whose name was to them unknown,) they did, for one night lend their nets to him, and that they received from him, on the following morning, a few herrings. This occurred but once, and for one night only; they never having remained in the islands for two consecutive nights.

The master of the American fishing schooner Magnolia, seized at the same time and place, deposed, in substance, to the same effect as the foregoing, except that they had not lent or parted with their nets. They deny most positively having fished, or attempted to take or catch fish, within fifteen miles of the coast of this province during the present season. The Magnolia is of the burden of thirty-seven tons, or thereabouts; belongs to Vinalhaven, and was fitted out and cleared from that port on a fishing voyage into the Bay of Fundy: she sailed from that port on the 26th day of April last, and was twice in the Tusket islands for shelter and for wood and water during the present season. The master's name is George Poole, the names of the seamen are William S. Coombs, David Lane and Samuel Clark, all residing at or near Vinalhaven, in the State of Maine.

The master of the schooner Java acknowledged that he and his crew had taken fish in the islands, and was aware that the fact of his having done so could be proved against him. We therefore declined to make any effort for his relief. The Java was fitted for a fishing voyage into the Bay of Fundy, and belonged to Vinalhaven; and she was seized at the same time and place as were the other two vessels before mentioned. Isaac Burgess was master; the crew were George McFarland, Charles J. Perkins and Thomas McFarland, all residing at or near Vinalhaven.

A few days subsequently, (on the 31st day of May last,) another application was made to me by James Turner, the master of the American fishing boat Hart, of Deer Island, in the State of Maine, who deposed that the boat was fitted out on a fishing voyage into the Bay of Fundy, about the last of April of the present year; that they had frequently been into the Tusket islands to seek shelter, and to obtain wood and water; and once only they anchored in this port, having come hither for the purpose of hiring an additional hand. They continued to fish until the 30th of May last, when, being at anchor in the Tusket islands, the vessel, cargo and papers were seized and taken possession of by the commander of the Victory, who brought the vessel and cargo into this port, and obliged the master and crew to leave her. They state most positively that they have not, since their departure from the port of Vinalhaven, taken or caught fish of any kind or description within fifteen miles of the coast of Nova Scotia, or of any of the other British coasts; nor did they at any one time remain in or among the said islands for a longer space of time than twenty-four hours. They state, however, that the master and Hiram Rich, one of the crew, did receive from Benjamin Brown, the master of a British fishing vessel at anchor in the said islands, about two barrels of herrings, given to them by Brown, to recompense them for their services in assisting him for one night at his request, in clearing his nets of herrings, salting and curing his fish.

This took place during one night that they came into the island for wood and water. This statement is corroborated on oath by Hiram Rich and Albert Douglass, two of the crew of this boat, and by —— Powers, a resident of this place, the additional hand above mentioned, who deposed to the truth of the statement of the master and crew, subsequent to the time of his engagement with them; before which time they had not proceeded to fish at all.

Benjamin Brown, a resident of Yarmouth, and a person of much respectability, deposes, that he first saw this vessel, the Hart, in the Tusket islands, on the first of May last; she having then but just arrived, as he believes, from Deer Island, and not having been in the islands before, during the present season. He further states, that afterwards this boat frequently came into the islands, at times when the state of the weather was such that the safety of the vessel and crew would have been endangered at sea; and at other times, as he believed, for wood and water, having frequently observed them proceed to the shore and bring therefrom a supply of those necessaries. He was, to the best of his belief, aware of the boat's arrival whenever she came into the islands, her place of anchorage being close to his vessel; and he says that the boat never remained in the said islands, at one time, for a longer space than twenty-four hours. He usually witnessed the boat get under weigh, and she always stood directly out to sea. He had frequent opportunities of observing the conduct of the master and crew of this boat, and he verily believes that no fish of any kind were taken by them in or near the said islands, subsequent to the 1st of May, the date of his arrival there; nor does he believe that they came there for the purpose of fishing or setting nets; and that, had they done so, he must have been aware of it, as the boat always anchored close to his vessel. He further stated that, at his request, the master of the boat and one of the crew named Rich, assisted him for one night in clearing his nets of herrings and in salting his fish, for which service he gave them two and a half barrels of herrings; and that he had seen the nets seized on board the boat, and that the meshes were too small to admit of the taking by them of any description of herring that had been upon the coast during the present season.

These depositions I enclosed to John Morrow, esquire, United States consul at Halifax, for the purpose of using them to assist him in his endeavors to effect the release of the Magnolia, Java and Hart, on the plea of their having been seized and detained on insufficient grounds.

The masters of these three last named vessels, by my advice proceeded to Halifax, where they now are awaiting the decision of the government officers there, whether they will be obliged to contest the legality of the seizures in the court of vice-admiralty at that place. I have received no information from thence that can be depended upon, as to the probable issue of the exertions already made and now making in behalf of the owners and others interested in these vessels.

The affidavits which have been made to substantiate the legality of these seizures are:

1. That of John McConnell, of this place, who deposes that he did see the crew of the Java, between the 11th and 27th days of May last, in the Tusket islands, put their nets into the boat belonging to that vessel, and on the following morning he saw them return with a quantity of fish, which was repeated four or five times during the above mentioned period; and that the skipper of the Java acknowledged to him that he had taken fish within the prohibited limits for bait. He further states that on Sunday, the 26th of May last, he saw on the deck of the Java, then lying in the Tusket islands, a quantity of gurry, which the crew said was from about three quintals of fish caught the day before, and that he, (the master,) and crew threw the same overboard, being then about two miles from Tebogue Point, in Yarmouth.

2. The same person, John McConnell, further deposed, that he saw the Magnolia, about two weeks previously, when at anchor in the islands, send two boats away in the evening with nets, and return again the next morning with fish; which also again took place for several successive days. He further stated, that the crew of the Magnolia did, about the same time, acknowledge that they were then taking fish among the Tusket islands, and had before been doing the same.

3. David McConnell, of Yarmouth, made oath that the skipper of the American schooner Independence acknowledged to him, on the 26th day of May, that he had hired nets belonging to that schooner to the skipper of an English fishing vessel, to be set by him on shares.

4. Jonathan Baker, of Yarmouth, deposed that between the 11th and 18th days of May last he saw the crew of the American schooner Java, then at anchor in the Tusket islands, put the nets out of the schooner into the boats in the evenings of four different days, leave the vessel, and return in the morning with the nets and a quantity of herring.

5. Joseph Darby, commander of the schooner Victory, deposed that he did see from on board the said schooner Victory, then lying in the Tusket islands, the crew of the American fishing-boat Hart cleaning fish on board of that vessel; and that the master of the Hart acknowledged to him that

he did about a week previously procure from Benjamin Brown two barrels of fresh herrings for bait.

The crew of the Magnolia positively deny the truth of the depositions made against them, and they say that their vessel must have been mistaken for some other. The crew of the Independence also deny having hired their nets. And it is probable that the acknowledgment sworn to as made by the masters has been misunderstood by the person to whom it was made; the real admission having been the lending the nets for one night to an inhabitant of the Tusket islands, as is mentioned in the deposition of the master and crew of the Independence. I need not remark upon the insufficiency of the evidence upon which the seizures of the Independence and Hart have been made. It consists entirely of verbal acknowledgments, which may be, and usually are misunderstood or misconstrued, and can seldom be correctly repeated; and indeed, taking for granted that the admissions sworn to have been made by the masters of these vessels, I cannot understand that they amount to evidence to authorize a seizure.

I may observe that these vessels have all been fitted out on shares; that is, each man on board in lieu of wages receives a share of fish at the termination of the voyage. This circumstance may be of importance, as it probably may affect their evidence in the court of vice-admiralty.

I have at present at this consulate two destitute American seamen of the boat Hart, (James Rich and Albert Douglas,) who, if not contrary to your instructions, I have to request that you will receive on board the cutter Hamilton, and land them at some convenient port in the United States.

The crews of the Java, Magnolia and Independence were put by me on board of a British schooner, the master of which landed them at Castine, in the State of Maine. They were in a perfectly destitute condition, the provisions and stores of the vessels having been seized. I had therefore to provide for them while they remained in this place, and to find them a passage to the United States.

I am, sir, your obedient, humble servant,

HENRY A. GRANTHAM,
Consular Agent U. S. for the Port of Yarmouth, N. S.

JOSIAH STURGIS, Esq.,
Commander of the American Revenue-cutter Hamilton.

CUSTOM-HOUSE, BOSTON, *June* 27, 1839.

I certify that the foregoing is a true copy from the original addressed to Captain Sturgis by Henry A. Grantham, Esq.

G. BANCROFT, *Collector.*

Circular instructions to officers of the customs residing in collection districts where vessels are licensed for employment in the fisheries of the United States.

TREASURY DEPARTMENT, *January* 21, 1836.

Representations have been made to our government through the chargé d'affaires of his Britannic Majesty, of encroachments by the American fishermen upon the fishing-grounds secured exclusively to British fishermen by the convention between the United States and Great Britain, bearing date the 20th day of October, 1818.

The President, being desirous of avoiding any just cause of dissatisfaction on the part of the British government on this subject, and with a view of preventing the injury which might result to the American fishermen from trespassing upon the acknowledged British fishing-grounds, directs that you will inform the masters, owners, and others employed in the fisheries in your district, of the foregoing complaints; and that they be enjoined to observe strictly the limits assigned for taking, drying, and curing fish, by the fishermen of the United States, under the convention before stated.

In order that persons engaged in the fisheries may be furnished with the necessary information, the first article of the convention, containing the provisions upon this subject, is annexed to this circular.

LEVI WOODBURY,
Secretary of the Treasury.

To the COLLECTOR OF ———.

P. S.—The collectors of Portland, Penobscot, Bath, Boston, Portsmouth, Gloucester and Newport are directed to publish these instructions twice a week for one month in each of the newspapers published at their respective ports, and charge the expenses as incidental to the collection of the revenue.

Extract from the convention with Great Britain of October 20, 1818.

"ARTICLE 1. Whereas differences have arisen respecting the liberty claimed by the United States for the inhabitants thereof, to take, dry and cure fish on certain coasts, bays, harbors and creeks of his Britannic majesty's dominions in America: it is agreed between the high contracting parties that the inhabitants of the said United States shall have forever, in common with the subjects of his Britannic Majesty, the liberty to take fish of every kind on that part of the southern coast of Newfoundland which extends from Cape Ray to the Rameau islands, on the western and northern coast of Newfoundland; from the said Cape Ray to the Quirpon islands, on the shores of the Magdalen islands; and also on the coasts, bays, harbors and creeks, from Mount Joly, on the southern coast of Labrador, to and through the straits of Belleisle; and thence northwardly, indefinitely, along the coast: without prejudice, however, to any of the exclusive rights of the Hudson Bay company. And that the American fishermen shall also have liberty forever to dry and cure fish in any part of the unsettled bays, harbors and creeks of the southern part of the coast of Newfoundland, here above described, and of the coast of Labrador; but so soon as the same, or any portion thereof shall be settled, it shall not be lawful for the said fishermen to dry or cure fish at such portion so settled, without previous agreement for such purpose with the inhabitants, proprietors, or possessors of the ground. And the United States hereby renounce forever any liberty heretofore enjoyed or claimed by the inhabitants thereof, to take, dry, or cure fish, on or within three marine miles of any of the coasts, bays, creeks or harbors of his Britannic Majesty's dominions in America, not included within the abovementioned limits: *Provided, however,* That the American fishermen shall be admitted to enter such bays or harbors for the purpose of shelter, and of repairing damages therein, of purchasing wood and of obtaining water, and for no other purpose whatever; but they shall be under such restrictions as may be necessary to prevent their taking, drying, or curing fish therein, or in any other manner whatever abusing the privileges reserved to them."

Acting Secretary of State to the President of the United States.

DEPARTMENT OF STATE,
August 14, 1839.

In obedience to the directions of the President, received at the Department of State on the 9th instant, "to report to him the treaty stipulations which bear upon the subject, (the seizure of American fishing vessels on the coast of Nova Scotia;) the conflicting questions of right, if any, which have arisen under them; and the nature and circumstances of the cases which have been presented to this government by our citizens, as infractions of right on the part of the British authorities," the acting Secretary of State has the honor to state:

That the only existing treaty stipulations bearing upon the subject are found in the first article of the convention between the United States and Great Britain, signed at London on the 20th of October, 1818, which is in the words following:

"Whereas differences have arisen respecting the liberty claimed by the United States for the inhabitants thereof to take, dry and cure fish on certain coasts, bays, harbors and creeks of his Britannic Majesty's dominions in America, it is agreed between the high contracting parties, that the inhabitants of the said United States shall have forever, in common with the subjects of his Britannic Majesty, the liberty to take fish of every kind on that part of the southern coast of Newfoundland which extends from Cape Ray to the Rameau islands; on the western and northern coast of Newfoundland, which extends from the said Cape Ray to the Quirpon islands; on the shores of the Magdalen islands; and also on the coasts, bays, harbors and creeks, from Mount Joly, on the southern coast of Labrador, to and through the straits of Belleisle; and thence northwardly, indefinitely, along the coast, without prejudice, however, to any of the exclusive rights of the Hudson Bay Company. And that the American fishermen shall also have liberty, forever, to dry and cure fish in any part of the unsettled bays, harbors and creeks of the southern part of the coast of Newfoundland, here above described, and of the coast of Labrador; but so soon as the same, or any portion thereof, shall be settled, it shall not be lawful for the said fishermen to dry or cure fish at such portion so settled, without previous agreement for such purpose with the inhabitants, proprietors, or possessors of the ground. And the United States hereby renounce forever, any liberty heretofore enjoyed or claimed by the inhabitants thereof to take, dry, or cure fish on or within three marine miles of any of the coasts, bays, creeks, or harbors of his Britannic Majesty's dominions in America, not included within the above mentioned limits: *Provided, however,* That the American fishermen shall be admitted to enter such bays or harbors for the purpose of shelter, and of repairing damages therein, of purchasing wood, and of obtaining water, and for no other purpose whatever; but they shall be under such restrictions as may be necessary to prevent their taking, drying, or curing fish therein, or in any other manner whatever abusing the privileges hereby reserved to them."

Under this article—

1. American vessels are allowed, forever, to take, dry, and cure fish on and along the coasts of Newfoundland and Labrador, within certain limits therein defined.

2. The United States renounce, forever, any liberty before enjoyed by their citizens to take fish within three marine miles of any coasts, bays, creeks, or harbors of the British dominions in America, not included within the above limits, *i. e.* Newfoundland and Labrador.

3. American vessels retain the privilege (under necessary restrictions to prevent their taking fish) of entering the bays, creeks, and harbors of said possessions, for the purposes of shelter, repairing damages, purchasing wood and obtaining water, and for no other purpose whatever.

It does not appear that the stipulations in the article above quoted have, since the date of the convention, been the subject of conflicting questions of right between the two governments. The rights of the respective parties are so clearly defined by the letter of the treaty, as scarcely to leave room for such questions of an abstract or general character. In their actual operation, however, inasmuch as their application on the part of Great Britain was to be subjected to local legislation, and committed to the hands of subordinate British agents, the provisions of the treaty might naturally be expected to give rise to difficulties growing out of individual acts on either side. The recent seizures appear to have had their origin in such causes, like other causes of anterior date, to which a brief allusion may here be useful.

In June, 1823, the Secretary of State addressed a note to the British minister at Washington, complaining of the seizure of the schooner Charles, and demanding reparation for the indignity offered to the American flag. The answer of the British government was, that the vessel had been found at anchor in a British harbor, which she had entered on a false pretence of avoiding a storm; and had been legally condemned by the vice-admiralty court of New Brunswick, for a breach of the convention of 1818, and of the act of Parliament to carry the same into effect. The vessel was subsequently restored.

In September, 1824, a complaint was made to the British chargé d'affaires that several citizens of the State of Maine had been interrupted by British cruisers, while engaged in taking and curing fish in the Bay of Fundy; and was accompanied by a similar demand of indemnity and reparation. The British chargé d'affaires, in answer, promised to institute an inquiry into the circumstances of the case, invited the United States to a similar proceeding on their part, and closed with a remonstrance against the act of American citizens who, with an armed force, had rescued the seized property from the custody of British officers.

In January, 1836, the British government became, in its turn, the complainant. Its chargé d'affaires at Washington, remonstrated against the encroachments of American citizens upon the fishing grounds secured exclusively to British fishermen by the convention of 1818. The result of this complaint was a circular letter addressed by the Secretary of the Treasury to the officers of customs in districts where vessels are licensed for the fisheries, directing them to impress the crews of fishing vessels with a sense of the treaty obligations of their government, and of the dangers to which they exposed themselves by encroaching upon British rights. The recent cases of seizure constitute the last instance of alleged violation of rights, and the charge is laid to the British account. The attention of this department was first called to the subject by a reference by the Treasury of a letter from B. & J. M. Leavitt, of Boston, asking for information as to the existing treaty stipulations regulating the matter. The inquiry was answered by a reference to the first article of the convention of 1818. On the 3d of July the Secretary of the Treasury referred to the department a communication from the collector of Boston, transmitting a report from the naval officer who had been despatched to Nova Scotia with directions to inquire into the alleged causes of the seizure and detention of American fishing vessels. The report, after alluding in general terms to some of the seizures, refers, with regard to the particulars of four of the cases then pending before the court of vice admiralty of Halifax, to an abridged statement, furnished by the consular agent of the United States at Yarmouth, of the depositions of the masters and crews of three American fishing schooners, viz: the "Independence," the "Magnolia," and the "Java," and the fishing boat "Hart." The statement, with the report accompanying it, is annexed, and contains the most detailed information in the possession of this department in relation to the "nature and circumstances of the cases."

According to that statement, the Independence is alleged to have anchored in the Tusket islands, and, while there, hired her nets to an English fisherman, for the purpose of taking fish on shares. The crew state that they were forced to anchor there by stress of weather; and that their nets had been lent, and not hired, for which they had received a few herrings.

The Magnolia is charged with having been engaged in fishing while at anchor in the Tusket islands, and with the fact having been acknowledged by the crew. This is denied; and the reason alleged for anchoring within British grounds is, want of shelter, wood and water.

The charge against the Java, of having been engaged in taking fish in the Tusket islands, is admitted by the master.

Against the Hart it is alleged that her crew were seen cleaning fish on board, while at anchor in the islands, and that her master had acknowledged that he had procured a quantity of herrings. The taking of fish is denied; and the fact of the crew having been seen cleaning fish is explained by stating that two barrels of herrings had been received from a British fisherman in recompense of services rendered.

On the 20th of July, a letter from the consul of the United States at Halifax, dated the 27th of June, was received at this department, informing it of the seizure of the four vessels above referred to, and of seven others, viz: the "Shetland," seized at Whitehead, near Canso; the "Charles," at Canso; the "Mayflower," and a schooner name unknown, at Guysborough; the "Battelle," "Hyder Ally," and "Eliza," at Beaver harbor.

The "Shetland" was seized on the ground of the master having sold to a lad who came on board, while the vessel lay at anchor in the harbor of Whitehead, whither she had been forced by stormy weather, a pair of oilcloth trousers, and small quantities of tea and tobacco. The master states in doing so he yielded to the importunities of the lad, whom he ›ves to have been sent purposely to entrap him into an attempt at ggling. He denies having caught fish within British limits.

/ith the exception of the "Eliza," which was likewise compelled to e a harbor by bad weather, and the crew of which deny having taken within the British limits, or having sold or bartered any articles what-, the particulars of the cases are not given; but in communications ressed by the consul to the Lieutenant Governor of Nova Scotia, asking interference in behalf of the owners of the seized vessels, he urges the rcise of indulgence and mercy, on the ground that some of the sufferers only erred in a slight degree either from ignorance or temptation, and hout intention to violate regulations, of the existence of which they ht, perhaps, never have heard.

'he communications from the consul to the Lieutenant Governor of va Scotia, having been referred to the advocate general of the Province, 'erwent examination, and a copy of his report accompanies the consul's er to the department. In this document, the advocate general denies power of the Governor to interfere or stay proceedings in the court of e admiralty, which alone has jurisdiction over the subject matter. He ls, that several of the cases had been commenced during his absence, l the evidence had not yet been submitted to him.

Commissions had been issued to take depositions in others. Three ves-s had been proceeded against by him, and the examination had proved t the crews of two of them had actually taken fish with set nets in Bea- harbor. In all other cases, where the evidence had not been submitted him, it was to be called for before any further proceedings were had. concludes by stating that, where the evidence is not complete, no decree ll be urged by default, until ample time and opportunity be afforded for fence, upon the most favorable terms that by law can be granted; and it in any case where there shall not appear good cause of prosecution, he ll exercise his own discretion in releasing the property.

From these statements it will appear that the only cases of seizure of ich anything is known at the department, not being made on the coasts Newfoundland or Labrador, occurred at places in which, under the con-ntion of 1818, the United States had forever renounced the right of their ssels to take, dry and cure fish; retaining only the privilege of entering em for the purposes of shelter, repairs, purchasing wood and obtaining ter, and no other. In the absence of information of a character suffi-ently precise to ascertain either, on the one side, the real motives which rried the American vessels into British harbors, or, on the other, the asons which induced their seizure by British authorities, the department unable to state whether, in the cases under consideration, there has been y flagrant infraction of the existing treaty stipulations. The presump-on is, that if, on the part of citizens of the United States, there has been want of caution or care in the strict observance of those stipulations, ere has been, on the other hand, an equal disregard of their spirit, and of e friendly relations which they were intended to promote and perpetuate, the haste and indiscriminate rigor with which the British authorities have ted.

Under the supposition that many of the seizures had been made upon sufficient grounds, and in order, if possible, to preclude for the future the currence of such proceedings, the acting Secretary of State, in a note dated the 10th of July, called the attention of the British minister to the cases of seizure which had come to the knowledge of the department, and requested him to direct the attention of the provincial authorities to the ruinous consequences of the seizures to the owners of the vessels, whatever might be the issue of the legal proceedings instituted against them; and to exhort them to exercise great caution and forbearance in future, in order that American citizens, not manifestly encroaching upon British rights, should not be subjected to interruption in the pursuit of their lawful avocations. The President's directions, that a vessel of war of suitable force should be held in readiness to proceed to the coasts of the British provinces having been communicated to the Secretary of the Navy, an answer has been received that the schooner Grampus, now lying at Norfolk, would be prepared to proceed to that quarter at a moment's notice; and that, should it be the desire of the President that a vessel of higher class should be employed on that duty, a sloop of war can be detailed from the station at Pensacola so as to be ready to sail at the end of this month.

Respectfully submitted.

A. VAIL,
Acting Secretary of State.

To the PRESIDENT *of the United States.*

Acting Secretary of State to Acting Secretary of the Navy.

DEPARTMENT OF STATE,
Washington, August 9, 1839.

SIR: Several seizures of fishing vessels belonging to citizens of the United States having been made by British cruisers in the harbors and along the coasts of Nova Scotia, the President has ordered an inquiry into the subject, and has directed me to inform your department that, for the purpose of protecting the rights and interests of our citizens in that quarter, a vessel of war, of suitable force, will soon be required to cruise off the coasts referred to.

I am, &c.

A. VAIL, *Acting Secretary.*

Commodore I. CHAUNCEY,
Acting Secretary of the Navy.

Acting Secretary of the Navy to Acting Secretary of State.

NAVY DEPARTMENT, *August* 9, 1839.

SIR: I have the honor to acknowledge the receipt of your letter of this date, apprising the department that, for the protection of the rights and interests of our citizens engaged in the fisheries along the coasts of Nova Scotia, a vessel of war will soon be required to cruise off these coasts; and to inform you that the United States schooner Grampus, now lying at Norfolk, will be prepared to proceed to that quarter with all practicable despatch, in obedience to the wishes of the President of the United States, as indicated by your letter.

I am, very respectfully, your obedient servant,

I. CHAUNCEY,
Acting Secretary of the Navy.

A. Vail, Esq.,
Acting Secretaay of State.

Acting Secretary of State to Acting Secretary of the Navy.

Department of State,
Washington, August 29, 1839.

Sir: In consequence of the recent seizure of several American vessels on the coast of Nova Scotia by the British colonial authorities, the President has determined that the schooner Grampus, which he deems sufficient for this service, shall be despatched to the coasts of the British provinces in the neighborhood of the fisheries, under the command of a judicious and competent officer, to be selected by the Secretary of the Navy, and furnished with instructions distinctly setting forth the rights of citizens of the United States under the treaty with Great Britain of the 20th of October, 1818, and making it his duty to protect them in the enjoyment of those rights, as well as to caution them against any infraction, on their part, of existing conventional stipulations. To enable you to carry these directions into effect, I have the honor to transmit to you, herewith, copies of papers containing all the information possessed by this department on the subject to which they relate; and, at the same time, to suggest that the consuls of the United States in the British provincial ports referred to, (to whom application may be made by the commander of the Grampus,) will, doubtless, cheerfully aid, by their advice, and by the communication of any pertinent facts within their knowledge, in advancing the objects of this visit.

I am, &c.,

A. VAIL, *Acting Secretary.*

Commodore Isaac Chauncey,
Acting Secretary of the Navy.

List of enclosures.

Report from the acting Secretary of State to the President, 14th of August, 1839.

Consul John Morrow to the Secretary of State (No. 77,) with enclosures, 27th of June, 1839.

Collector Bancroft to the Secretary of the Treasury, with enclosures, 27th of June, 1839.

Acting Secretary of the Navy to acting Secretary of State.

NAVY DEPARTMENT, *August* 30, 1839.

SIR: Your letter of yesterday's date, stating the determination of the President that the schooner Grampus shall be despatched to the coasts of the British provinces in the neighborhood of the fisheries, under the command of a judicious and competent officer, to be selected by the Secretary of the Navy, and furnished with instructions distinctly setting forth the rights of citizens of the United States under the treaty with Great Britain of October, 1818, and making it his duty to protect them in the enjoyment of those rights, as well as to caution them against any infraction, on their part, of existing conventional stipulations, has been received, together with the copies of documents therewith transmitted.

The schooner Grampus is ready for sea, and shall be despatched, in accordance with the determination of the President, as soon as the necessary instructions can be prepared and transmitted to her commander.

I am, very respectfully, your obedient servant,

I. CHAUNCY,
Acting Secretary of the Navy.

A. VAIL, Esq.,
Acting Secretary of State.

Acting Secretary of the Navy to the Secretary of State.

NAVY DEPARTMENT, *September* 4, 1839.

SIR: Lieutenant John S. Paine, commanding the United States schooner Grampus, was yesterday ordered to proceed, without delay, to the coasts of the British provinces, in obedience to the directions of the President communicated to this department by the Department of State on the 29th ult.

I am, very respectfully, your obedient servant,

I. CHAUNCEY,
Acting Secretary of the Navy.

HON. JOHN FORSYTH,
Secretary of State.

Lieutenant Commanding Paine to Mr. Forsyth.

WASHINGTON, *December* 29, 1839.

SIR: In my late cruise on the coasts of her Britannic Majesty's provinces, I found the convention of 1818, on the subject of fisheries, so variously construed, that I deemed it proper to address the Navy Department on the subject—the letters to which I alluded in conversation with you.

Avoiding unnecessary repetitions, I will endeavor to give, in the following, all that seems of importance in a more concise form.

I visited the seat of government of Nova Scotia, and that of Prince Edward's Island, and St. John's, the principal city of New Brunswick, wher I communicated with the principal government officers, with our consuls, with Admiral Sir Thomas Harvey, and the commanders of the British vessels of war with whom I met; as also with the collectors of Portland and Eastport, Maine, and such other persons as from their situations seemed qualified to impart information on the questions arising.

I had believed the vessels seized had been generally guilty of systematic violation of the revenue laws; but I was soon led to suspect that this was not the cause, so much as a pretence, for seizing.

A vessel once seized must be condemned, unless released as a favor; because the owners will not claim her under the present laws of Nova Scotia, where the only seizures have taken place.

The questions on which dispute may arise, are—

1*st*. The meaning of the word *bay*, in the convention of 1818, where the Americans relinquish the rights before claimed or exercised, of fishing in or upon any of the coasts, *bays*, &c., of her Britannic Majesty's provinces, not before described, nearer than three miles.

The authorities of Nova Scotia seem to claim a right to exclude Americans from all bays, including those large seas such as the Bay of Fundy and the Bay of Chaleurs; and also to draw a line from headland to headland; the Americans not to approach within three miles of this line.

The fishermen, on the contrary, believe they have a right to work anywhere, if not nearer than three miles to the land.

The orders of Admiral Sir Thomas Harvey, as he informed me, are only to prevent their fishing nearer than three miles.

According to this construction, Americans may fish in the Bay of Fundy, Bay of Chaleurs, and the Bay of Miramichi; while their right would be doubtful in Chedabucto bay, and they would be prohibited in the other bays of Nova Scotia.

On that part of the coast of Newfoundland where the right of fishing is relinquished, there are several bays in which fisheries may be prosecuted at three or more miles from the land.

On that part of the coast of Newfoundland where the right of taking and curing fish is secured by the convention of 1818, it is to be feared that troubles may arise with the French, who assume an exclusive right, and who have gone so far as to drive off even English fishermen.

The right of fishing on the shores of the Magdalen islands, though sometimes questioned, seems so secured by the convention of 1818 that I think it unnecessary to lengthen this communication by further discussing it.

2*d*. The right of resorting to ports for shelter, and to procure wood and water. The provincial authorities claim a right to exclude vessels, unless in actual distress; and the subordinates, as well as the naval forces of her Majesty, warn, as they term it, vessels to depart, or order them to get under weigh and leave a harbor when they suppose a vessel has lain a reasonable time; but this is often done without examining or knowing much of the circumstances under which the vessel entered, or how long she has been in port.

The English men-of-war also endorse the papers of the fishermen, as if they had violated the blockade, or committed some other illegal act.

The fishermen claim a right, under the convention, to resort to the ports for shelter whenever from rough weather, calms or fogs, they cannot prosecute, without risk or inconvenience, their labors at sea; and the navigation on some parts of the coast is, on account of the extraordinary tides, as perilous in calms and fogs as in rough weather.

The Nova Scotia courts would exact that American fishermen shall have been supplied, on leaving home, with wood and water for the cruise; but the Americans believe they can, by the terms of the convention, resort to the ports to procure wood and water at their convenience during the cruise; and they do not, on account of the inconvenience, as well as the high price, take on board either water-casks or wood for the whole cruise.

If the grounds assumed by the British provincial authorities be carried out, it will be in their power to drive the Americans from those parts of the coast where are some of the most valuable fisheries: whereas, if the ground maintained by the Americans be admitted, it will be difficult to prevent their procuring articles of convenience, and particularly bait; from which they are precluded by the convention, and which a party in the provinces seems resolved to prevent.

The questions will, I doubt not, ere long be brought to a crisis; and it seems probable that the vexatious course pursued towards the fishermen, with the object of fostering their own at the expense of our fisheries, and the care taken by the French to protect and encourage theirs, will tend to injure, perhaps destroy those of this country; a result to be deprecated in connexion with the navy, for there is no branch of commerce which supplies so large a portion of hardy and efficient seamen.

Although several of the vessels seized by authority of the province of Nova Scotia were afterwards released, the great expense incurred and the time they were detained made the injury to the owners nearly equal to a total loss.

The person who made the most of these seizures, (a Mr. Darby, who commands a chebacco boat, with ten or twelve men armed with muskets,) is prompted, as well by his interest as by a certainty of impunity, to seize all he can find.

The law of this province, entitled William IV, chap. viii, 1836, which seems solely intended to prosecute our fishermen, could only have been approved by orders in council through an oversight.

It is not possible that Great Britain intends, when the property of citizens of a nation in amity is seized on false pretences, or with no pretence, to force the lawful owner to give heavy bonds, liable to be forfeited, in addition to vessel and cargo, before he can claim his property:

To give a month's notice to the seizing officer; the notice to contain every thing intended to be proved against him, before a suit can be instituted; and, again, to prove that the notice has been given:

To force the owner to bring his action or claim within three months—one of which is expended in thus giving notice, and the other two may well expire, owing to the infrequency and uncertainty of communications, before the distant owner can transfer funds and give the requisite bonds to precede his suit, or lay claim to his illegally seized property, which property will thus be condemned by default:

To force the owner, if he cannot prove the illegality of the seizure, to pay treble costs:

To screen the officer seizing, by providing that, if the judge shall say there was probable cause, he shall be liable to no prosecution; the plaintiff only entitled to second damages; the defendant only liable to costs.

The whole of this act, and the proceedings on the subject, as detailed in the journals of the assembly, display an unfriendly disposition towards

Americans, or rather a determination to quarrel or drive them from the exercise of rights secured by solemn treaty.

The injustice and annoyance sufferred by the fishermen have so irritated them, that there is ground to believe that violence will be resorted to, unless some understanding be had before the next season.

As the facts relating to these seizures have been reported to the government by Messrs. Consuls Morrow, of Halifax, and Primrose, of Pictou, I have confined myself to such a representation of the grounds assumed as may be useful in judging of the danger of serious difficulty, which has seemed to me considerable.

There is another law of this province, unjust towards foreigners, and likely to be injurious to Americans. It relates to passenger-vessels which may be forced from any cause to make a harbor, and is entitled 1st Victoria, 1839, chapter xlv., sections 3 and 5.

If any of the passengers please, they may remain on shore, and the vessel will not be cleared until bonds are given to the amount of £50 for each person so remaining that they shall not become chargeable to the community; and this, while the captain is willing or desirous of finishing his contract by conveying them to their destination.

At Prince Edward's island, the schooner Three Brothers, of Belfast, having met with some injury by grounding, commenced lightening; but the captain was advised to apply for permission, and did so; the permission was refused, and the articles landed (some barrels of salt) were seized.

This was afterwards ordered to be restored to the owners, but had already been sold; and the proceeds are now in the hands of the collector of customs at Charlottetown, subject to the orders of the honorable the board of customs in London, and cannot be claimed by the owners without first entering into bonds—probable ten times the amount of the salt seized.

I believe that a consul, to reside at Charlottetown, with the usual power of appointing agents, would be a means of preventing future difficulties; the only intercourse with the authorities now being through a consular agent appointed by Consul James Primrose, of Pictou, in another province.

I have the honor to subscribe myself, with high respect, your obedient servant,

JNO. S. PAINE,
Lieut. Comd'g U. S. schooner Grampus.

Hon. John Forsyth,
Secretary of State.

ILLEGAL SEIZURE OF AMERICAN FISHING VESSELS.

Message from the President of the United States, communicating, in compliance with a resolution of the Senate, information of measures taken to obtain redress from the British government for the illegal capture of American vessels engaged in the fisheries.

IN SENATE, *March* 3, 1845.
Read and laid on the table.

To the Senate of the United States:

I transmit herewith to the Senate, in answer to its resolution of the 17th instant, a report from the Secretary of State, together with the copies of papers therein referred to.

JOHN TYLER.

WASHINGTON, *February* 28, 1845.

DEPARTMENT OF STATE,
Washington, February 28, 1845.

The Secretary of State, to whom has been referred the resolution of the Senate of the 17th instant, requesting the President to inform that body, if not incompatible with the public interest, "what measures, if any, have been taken by the government of the United States to obtain redress from the British government for the illegal capture of the fishing schooner "Argus," of Portland, and other American vessels engaged in the fisheries, under a pretended infraction of the convention of 20th October, 1818," has the honor to report to the President the accompanying copies and extracts of correspondence, from the files of the department, embracing the information called for.

Respectfully submitted,
J. C. CALHOUN.

To the PRESIDENT OF THE UNITED STATES.

LIST OF ACCOMPANYING PAPERS.

Acting Secretary of State to Mr. Fox, July 10, 1839.
Mr. Forsyth to Mr. Fox, July 24, 1839.
Mr. Forsyth to Mr. Stevenson, February 20, 1841.
Mr. Stevenson to Mr. Webster, April 7, 1841. (Extract.)
Same to same, May 18, 1841. (Extract.)
Mr. Upshur to Mr. Everett, June 30, 1843.
Mr. Everett to Mr. Upshur, August 15, 1843. (Extract.)
Same to Mr. Calhoun, May 26, 1844. (Extract.)
Mr. Calhoun to Mr. Everett, July 5, 1844. (Extract.)
Same to same, September 6, 1844.
Mr. Everett to Mr. Calhoun, October 9, 1844. (Extracts.)
Same to same, November 4, 1844.

Acting Secretary of State to Mr. Fox.

DEPARTMENT OF STATE,
Washington, July 10, 1839.

SIR: I have the honor to communicate to you copies of papers* referred to this department by the Secretary of the Treasury, respecting the seizure of several fishing boats belonging to citizens of the United States, by the British government vessel "Victory," in the Bay of Fundy, on a charge of having been engaged in taking fish within British jurisdiction, contrary to existing treaty stipulations between the United States and Great Britain, and the laws of the Province of Nova Scotia.

You will perceive from these papers, that, in the opinion of the naval officer despatched by the collector of customs at Boston to inquire into the circumstances of the seizures, and of the consular agent of the United States at Yarmouth, who had been desired to furnish the information in his possession on the subject, some, at least, of those seizures were made for causes of a trivial character, and with a rigor not called for by circumstances. Not doubting that justice will ultimately be done to the sufferers by the colonial courts in which proceedings have been instituted against them, my object in addressing this communication to you is to invoke your good offices in calling the attention of her Majesty's provincial authorities to the ruinous consequences of those seizures to our fishermen, whatever may be the issue of the legal proceedings founded upon them, and to the consequent expediency of great caution and forbearance in future, in order that American citizens, not manifestly encroaching upon British rights, be not subjected to interruption in the lawful pursuit of their profession.

I have the honor, &c.,

A. VAIL, *Acting Secretary.*

HENRY S. FOX, Esq., &c., &c.

Mr. Forsyth to Mr. Fox.

DEPARTMENT OF STATE,
Washington, July 24, 1839.

SIR: I have the honor to communicate to you a copy of a letter† addressed to this department by the collector of customs of the district of Frenchman's bay, asking its interposition in obtaining for Captain Benjamin S. Moore, of the fishing schooner "Charles," the restitution of ten barrels of herrings taken from him by the officer who seized his vessel, and still withheld after her release by the authorities of Halifax. As the vessel was given up, it is presumed that the seizure had been made upon insufficient grounds, and therefore, that upon the institution of legal proceedings, Captain Moore would obtain the restitution of the property still withheld from him. As it seems, however, that he is poor, that he has already suffered a heavy loss in consequence of the detention of his vessel, and consequently that he could but ill bear the expense and delay attending such

---

* See House Document No. 186, 26th Congress, 1st session, pp. 85—92 of this document.

† Ibid., p. 82.

legal proceedings, I request that you will use your good offices with the authorities of Halifax to procure for the claimant either the return of his property or such indemnity for the loss of it as may seem reasonable and just.

I have the honor, &c.,

JOHN FORSYTH.

HENRY S. FOX, Esq., &c., &c., &c.

Mr. Forsyth to Mr. Stevenson.

DEPARTMENT OF STATE,
[No. 89.] *Washington, February* 20, 1841.

SIR: At the time of addressing you the instructions numbered 71, of 17th of April last, relating to the interruptions experienced by the vessels of our citizens employed in intercourse with the ports of Nova Scotia, and in the prosecution of the fisheries on the neighboring coasts, it was deemed expedient, before presenting through you the latter branch of the subject to her Majesty's government in a formal manner, to await the communication to this department of a case in which the details of the seizure—the grounds on which it was made, and the consequent judicial and other proceedings should be fully set forth. Several cases of seizures and detention have, as was apprehended, occurred since the date of my letter, but none of those reported to the department have been presented in a form to fulfil the expectation entertained that the government would be enabled to found upon it a specific complaint against the conduct of the local authorities, whilst protesting against the injurious operation of provincial law upon American interests brought involuntarily and unjustly within its jurisdiction.

The first article of the convention of 1818, between the United States and Great Britain, which contains the treaty stipulations relating to the subject, is so explicit in its terms that there would seem to be little room for misapprehending them; and indeed it does not appear that any conflicting questions of right between the two governments have arisen out of differences of opinion between them regarding the intent and meaning of this article. Yet in the actual application of the provisions of the treaty, committed, on the part of Great Britain, to the hands of subordinate agents, subject to and controlled by local legislation, difficulties growing out of individual acts have sprung up from time to time, and of these, perhaps the most grave in their character, are the recent seizures of American vessels, made, it is believed, under color of a provincial law, entitled William IV., chap. 8, 1836, enacted doubtless with a view rigorously to restrict, if not intended directly to aim a fatal blow at our fisheries on the coast of Nova Scotia.

From the information in the possession of the department, it appears that the provincial authorities assume a right to exclude American vessels from all their bays, even including those of Fundy and Chaleurs, and to prohibit their approach within three miles of a line drawn from headland to headland.

These authorities also claim a right to exclude our vessels from resorting to their ports unless in actual distress, and American vessels are accordingly warned to depart or ordered to get under weigh and leave a harbor whenever the provincial custom-house or British naval officer supposes, without a full examination of the circumstances under which they entered, that they have been there a reasonable time.

Now, by the convention above referred to, American fishermen are forever secured in their right to take, dry, and cure fish on the coasts of the Magdalen islands and of Newfoundland and Labrador, within certain defined limits, and the United States renounced forever any liberty before enjoyed by their citizens of fishing within three marine miles of any coasts, bays, &c., of the British domains in America not included within those limits, and retain for their vessels the privilege (under the restrictions therein named,) of entering such bays or harbors for the purposes of shelter, and of repairing damages therein, of purchasing wood, and of obtaining water.

Our fishermen believe, and they are obviously right in their opinion, if uniform practice is any evidence of correct construction, that they can with propriety take fish anywhere on the coasts of the British provinces, if not nearer than three miles to land, and resort to their ports for shelter, wood, water, &c.; nor has this claim ever been seriously disputed, based as it is on the plain and obvious terms of the convention, whilst the construction attempted to be put upon that instrument by the authorities of Nova Scotia is directly in conflict with its provisions, and entirely subversive of the rights and interests of our citizens. It is one which would lead to the abandonment, to a great extent, of a highly important branch of American industry, and cannot for one moment be admitted by this government.

I am instructed by the President to convey to you his desire that, on the receipt of this letter, you immediately address a representation of the whole subject to her Majesty's government, earnestly remonstrate against the illegal and vexatious proceedings of the authorities of Nova Scotia towards our fishermen, and request that measures be forthwith adopted by her Majesty's government to remedy the evils arising out of this misconstruction, on the part of the provincial authorities, of their conventional obligations, and to prevent the possibility of the recurrence of similar acts.

It is important that this subject should be acted upon without delay, as in the House of Assembly of Nova Scotia, at the session of 1839–'40, an address to the Queen was voted, suggesting the extension to the adjoining British colonies, of rules and regulations relating to the fisheries similar to those in actual operation in that province, which have proved so onerous to American fishermen, and efforts, it is understood, are still making to induce the other colonies to unite with Nova Scotia in her restrictive system. Some of the provisions of her code, supposed to be substantially the same with those of the provincial law above referred to, are of the most extraordinary character. For instance, a foreign vessel *preparing* to fish within three miles of the coast of her Majesty's dominions in America, is, together with her cargo, to be forfeited; in cases of seizure the owner or claimant of the vessel, &c., to be held to prove his innocence or pay treble costs; he is forced to try his action within three months; to give a month's notice to the seizing officer, which notice must contain everything intended to be proved against him, before a suit can be instituted; and also to prove that the notice has been given. The seizing officer is almost wholly irresponsible, since he is liable to no prosecution; if the judge certify that there was probable cause, and the plaintiff in such suit, if he be successful, is only entitled to two pence damages without costs, the defendant to be fined not more than one shilling, &c., &c. In short, some of these rules and regulations are violations of well established principles of the common law of England and of the principles of all just powers and all civilized nations, and seem to be expressly designed to enable her Majesty's authorities, with perfect impunity, to seize and confiscate American vessels, and to embezzle, almost indiscriminately, the property of our citizens employed in the fisheries on the coasts of the British possessions.

In pointing out to her Majesty's government the points in these regulations which have proved or are likely to prove most injurious and oppressive in their practical operation on the interests of the citizens of the United States, it will also be proper to notice the assertion of the provincial legislature, that the Strait of Canso is a "narrow strip of water completely within and dividing several counties" of the province, and that our use of it is in violation of the convention of 1818. That strait separates Nova Scotia from the island of Cape Breton, which was not annexed to the province until 1820. In 1818, Cape Breton was enjoying a government of its own entirely distinct from Nova Scotia, the strait forming the line of demarcation between them, and being then, as now, a thoroughfare for vessels passing into and out of the Gulf of St. Lawrence. The union of the two colonies cannot be admitted as vesting in the province the right to close a passage which has been freely and indisputably used by our citizens since the year 1783, and it is impossible to conceive how the use, on our part, of this right of passage, common it is believed to all other nations, conflicts either with the letter or the spirit of our treaty obligations.

I transmit to you enclosed a printed House document (No. 186) of last session of Congress, and also a copy of the journal and proceedings of the House of Assembly of Nova Scotia at its session of 1839–40, both of which will be useful to you in the examination of the subject to which this letter relates.

I am, sir, your obedient servant,

JOHN FORSYTH.

A. STEVENSON, &c., &c., &c.

CHAP. VIII.—*An act relating to the fisheries, and for the prevention of illicit trade in the province of Nova Scotia and the coasts and harbors thereof, passed the 12th day of March*, 1836.

Whereas, by the convention made between his late Majesty, King George the Third, and the United States of America, signed at London on the twentieth day of October, in the year of our Lord one thousand eight hundred and eighteen, and the statute made and passed in the Parliament of Great Britain in the fifty-ninth year of the reign of his late Majesty, King George the Third, all foreign ships, vessels or boats, or any ship, vessel or boat, other than such as shall be navigated according to the laws of the United Kingdom of Great Britain and Ireland, found fishing, or to have been fishing, or preparing to fish within certain distances of any coasts, bays, creeks or harbors whatever, in any part of his Majesty's dominions in America not included within the limits specified in the first article of the said convention, are liable to seizure: and whereas the United States did, by the said convention, renounce forever any liberty enjoyed or claimed by the inhabitants thereof to take, dry or cure fish on or within three marine miles of any of the coasts, bays, creeks or harbors of his Britannic Majesty's dominions in America not included within the above mentioned limits: *Provided, however*, That the American fishermen should be admitted to enter such bays or harbors for the purpose of shelter, and of repairing damages therein, of purchasing wood and of obtaining water, and for no other purpose whatever, but under such restrictions as might be necessary to prevent their taking, drying or curing fish therein, or in any other manner whatever abusing the privileges thereby reserved to them: and whereas no rules or regulations have been made for such purpose, and the interests of the inhabitants of this province are materially impaired; and whereas the said act does not designate the persons who are to make such seizure as aforesaid, and it frequently happens that persons found within the distances of the coasts aforesaid, infringing the articles of the convention aforesaid, and the enactments of the statute aforesaid, on being taken possession of, profess to have come within said limits for the purpose of shelter and repairing damages therein, or to purchase wood and obtain water, by which the law is evaded, and the vessels and cargoes escape confiscation, although the cargoes may be evidently intended to be smuggled into this province, and the fishery carried on contrary to said convention and statute.

I. *Be it therefore enacted by the Lieutenant Governor, Council and Assembly*, That from and after the passage of this act, it shall be lawful for the officers of his Majesty's customs, the officers of impost and excise, the sheriffs and magistrates throughout the province, and any person holding a commission for that purpose from his excellency the Lieutenant Governor, for the time being, to go on board any ship, vessel or boat, within any port, bay, creek or harbor in this province; and also, to go on board of any ship, vessel or boat, hovering within three marine miles of any of the coasts, bays, creeks or harbors thereof, and in either case freely to stay on board such ship, vessel or boat, as long as she shall remain within such port or distance; and if any such ship, vessel or boat be bound elsewhere, and shall continue so hovering for the space of twenty-four hours after the master shall have been required to depart, it shall be lawful for any of the above enumerated officers or persons to bring such ship, vessel or boat into port, and to search and examine her cargo, and to examine the master on oath touching the cargo and voyage, and if there be any goods on board prohibited to be imported into the province, such ship, vessel or boat, and the cargo laden on board thereof, shall be forfeited; and if the said ship, vessel or boat shall be foreign, and not navigated according to the laws of Great Britain and Ireland, and shall have been found fishing or preparing to fish, or to have been fishing within such distance of such coasts, bays, creeks or harbors of this province, such ship, vessel or boat, and their respective cargoes, shall be forfeited; and if the master, or person in command thereof, shall not truly answer the questions which shall be demanded of him in such examination, he shall forfeit the sum of one hundred pounds.

II. *And be it further enacted*, That all goods, ships, vessels and boats liable to forfeiture under this act, shall and may be seized and secured by any such officer of his Majesty's customs, officer of impost and excise, sheriffs, magistrates or other person holding such commission, as aforesaid; and every person who shall in any way oppose, molest or obstruct any officer of the customs, officers of impost and excise, sheriff, magistrate, or other person so commissioned and employed as aforesaid, in the exercise of his office, or shall in any way oppose, molest or obstruct any person acting in aid or assistance of such officer of the customs, officers of impost and excise, sheriff, magistrate, or other person so commissioned and employed as aforesaid, shall, for every such offence, forfeit the sum of two hundred pounds.

III. *And be it further enacted,* That all goods, ships, vessels and boats which shall be seized as being liable to forfeiture under this act, shall be taken forthwith and delivered into the custody of the collector and comptroller of the customs, at the custom-house next to the place where the same were seized, who shall secure and keep the same in such manner as other vessels and goods seized are directed to be secured by the commissioners of his Majesty's customs.

IV. *And be it further enacted,* That all goods, ships, vessels, boats or other thing, which shall have been condemned as forfeited under this act, shall, under the direction of the principal officer of the customs or excise where such seizures shall have been secured, be sold by public auction to the best bidder, and the produce of such sale shall be applied as follows, that is to say: the amount chargeable for the custody of said goods, ship, vessel, boat or any other thing so seized as aforesaid, shall be first deducted and paid, and the residue divided into two equal moieties, one of which shall be paid to the officer or other person or persons legally seizing the same, without deduction, and the other moiety to the government, and paid into the treasury of this province, all costs incurred having been first deducted therefrom. *Provided always,* That it shall be lawful for the commissioners of the revenue to direct that any of such things shall be destroyed or reserved for the public service.

V. *And be it further enacted,* That all penalties and forfeitures which may be hereafter incurred under this act, shall and may be prosecuted, sued for and recovered in the court of vice-admiralty having jurisdiction in this province.

VI. *And be it further enacted,* That if any goods, or any ship, vessel or boat, shall be seized as forfeited under this act, it shall be lawful for the judge or judges of any court having jurisdiction to try and determine such seizures, with the consent of the person seizing the same, to order the delivery thereof, on security by bond, with two sufficient sureties to be first approved by such seizing officer or person, to answer double the value of the same in case of condemnation, and such bond shall be taken to the use of his Majesty, in the name of the collector of the customs in whose custody the goods or ship, vessel or boats may be lodged, and such bond shall be delivered and kept in the custody of such collector; and in case the goods or the ship, vessel or boat shall be condemned, the value thereof shall be paid into the hands of such collector, who shall cancel such bond, and distribute the money paid in such manner as above directed.

VII. *And be it further enacted,* That no suit shall be commenced for the recovery of any penalty or forfeiture under this act, except in the name of his Majesty, and shall be prosecuted by his Majesty's advocate or attorney general, or, in his absence, by the solicitor general for this province; and if any question shall arise, whether any person is an officer of the customs or excise, sheriff, magistrate, or other person authorised to seize as aforesaid, *viva voce* evidence may be given of such facts, and shall be deemed legal and sufficient evidence.

VIII. *And be it further enacted*, That if any goods, ship, vessel or boat shall be seized for any cause or forfeiture under this act, and any dispute shall arise whether the same have been lawfully seized, the proof touching the illegality thereof shall lie on the owner or claimant of such goods, ship, vessel or boat, and not on the officer or person who shall seize and stop the same.

IX. *And be it further enacted*, That no claim to anything seized under this act, and returned into his Majesty's court of vice-admiralty for adjudication, shall be admitted, unless such claim be entered in the name of the owner, with his residence and occupation, nor unless oath to the property in such thing be made by the owner or by his attorney or agent by whom such claim shall be entered, to the best of his knowledge and belief; and every person making a false oath thereto shall be deemed guilty of a misdemeanor, and shall be liable to the pains and penalties to which persons are liable for a misdemeanor.

X. *And be it further enacted*, That no person shall be admitted to enter a claim to anything seized in pursuance of this act, and prosecuted in this Province, until sufficient security shall have been given in the court where such seizure is prosecuted, in a penalty not exceeding sixty pounds, to answer and pay the costs occasioned by such claim; and in default of giving such security, such things shall be adjudged to be forfeited, and shall be condemned.

XI. *And be it further enacted*, That no writ shall be sued out against, nor a copy of any process served upon any officer of the customs or excise, sheriff, magistrate, or other person authorized to seize as aforesaid, for anything done in the exercise of his office, until one calendar month after notice in writing shall have been delivered to him or left at his usual place of abode by the attorney or agent of the party who intends to sue out such writ or process, in which notice shall be clearly and explicitly contained the cause of action, the name and place of abode of the person who is to bring such action, and the name and place of abode of the attorney or agent, and no evidence of the cause of such action shall be produced, except of such as shall be contained in such notice, and no verdict shall be given for the plaintiff unless he shall prove on the trial that such notice was given; and in default of such proof, the defendant shall receive in such action a verdict and costs, or judgment of nonsuit shall be awarded against the plaintiff, as the court shall direct.

XII. *And be it further enacted*, That every such action shall be brought within three calendar months after the cause thereof, and shall be laid and tried in any of his Majesty's courts of record in this Province, and the defendant may plead the general issue, and give the special matter in evidence; and, if the plaintiff shall become nonsuited, or shall discontinue the action, or if, upon a verdict or demurrer, judgment shall be given against the plaintiff, the defendent shall receive treble costs, and have such remedy for the same as any defendant can have in other cases where costs are given by law.

XIII. *And be it further enacted*, That in case any information or suit shall be brought to trial on account of any seizure made under this act, and a verdict shall be found for the claimant thereof, and the judge or court before whom the cause shall have been tried shall certify on the record that there was probable cause of seizure, the claimant shall not be entitled to any costs of suit, nor shall the person who made such seizure be liable to any action. Indictment, or other suit or prosecution on account of such seizure, and if any action, indictment or other suit or prosecution shall be brought to trial against any person on account of such seizure, wherein a verdict shall be given against the defendant, the plaintiff, besides the thing seized, or the value thereof, shall be entitled to no more than two pence damages, nor to any costs of suit, nor shall the defendent in such prosecution be fined more than one shilling.

XIV. *And be it further enacted*, That it shall be lawful for any such officer of the customs or excise, or sheriff, or magistrate, or other person authorised to seize as aforesaid, within one calendar month after such notice, to tender amends to the party complaining, or his agent, and to plead such tender in bar to any action, together with other pleas; and if the jury shall find the amends sufficient they shall give a verdict for the defendant; and, in such case, or in case the plaintiff shall become nonsuit, or shall discontinue his action, or judgment shall be given for the defendant upon demurrer, then such defendant shall be entitled to the like costs as he would have been entitled to in case he had pleaded the general issue only: *Provided always*, That it shall be lawful for such defendant, by leave of the court where such action shall be brought, at any time before or after issue joined, to pay money into court as in other actions.

XV. *And be it further enacted*, That in any such action, if the judge or court before whom such action shall be tried, shall certify upon the record that the defendant or defendants in such action acted upon probable cause, then the plaintiff in such action shall not be entitled to more than two pence damages, nor to any costs of suit.

XVI. *And be it further enacted*, That all actions or suits for the recovery of any of the penalties or forfeitures imposed by this act, may be commenced or prosecuted at any time within three years after the offence committed, by reason whereof such penalty or forfeiture shall be incurred, any law, usage or custom to the contrary notwithstanding.

XVII. *And be it further enacted*, That no appeal shall be prosecuted from any decree or sentence of any of his Majesty's courts in this province, touching any penalty or forfeiture imposed by this act, unless the inhibition shall be applied for and decreed within twelve months from the time when such decree or sentence was pronounced.

XVIII. *And be it further enacted*, That this act shall not go into force or be of any effect until his Majesty's assent shall be signified thereto, and an order made by his Majesty, in council, that the clauses and provisions of this act shall be the rules, regulations and restrictions respecting the fisheries on the coasts, bays, creeks or harbors of the province of Nova Scotia.

[Extract.]

Mr. Stevenson to Mr. Webster.

LEGATION OF THE UNITED STATES,
London, April 7, 1841.

* * * * * * * * *

I received on the 22d of March Mr. Forsyth's despatch of the 20th of February, on the subject of the fisheries and the intercourse of our vessels with Nova Scotia. * * * * * I immediately addressed an official note to Lord Palmerston on the subject of the fisheries, a copy of which, with his Lordship's acknowledgement, I have now the honor to enclose.

[Enclosure.]

Mr. Stevenson to Lord Palmerston.

32 UPPER GROSVENOR STREET,
March 27, 1841.

The undersigned, Envoy Extraordinary and Minister Plenipotentiary from the United States, has the honor to acquaint Lord Viscount Palmerston, her Majesty's Principal Secretary of State for Foreign Affairs, that he has been instructed to bring to the notice of her Majesty's government, without delay, certain proceedings of the colonial authorities of Nova Scotia, in relation to the seizure and interruption of the vessels and citizens of the United States engaged in intercourse with the ports of Nova Scotia, and the prosecution of the fisheries on its neighboring coasts, and which, in the opinion of the American government, demand the prompt interposition of her Majesty's government. For this purpose the undersigned takes leave to submit to Lord Palmerston the following representation:

By the first article of the convention between Great Britain and the United States, signed at London, on the 20th of October, 1818, it is provided: "1st. That the inhabitants of the United States shall have forever, in common with the subjects of Great Britain, the liberty to take fish of every kind on that part of the southern coast of Newfoundland which extends from Cape Ray to the Rameau islands; on the western and northern coast of Newfoundland, from the said Cape Ray to the Quirpon islands; on the shores of the Magdalen islands; and also on the coasts, bays, harbors and creeks from Mount Joly, on the southern coast of Labrador, to and through the straits of Belleisle, and thence northwardly indefinitely along the coast, without prejudice, however, to the exclusive rights of the Hudson Bay Company. 2dly. That the American fishermen shall also have liberty forever to dry and cure fish in any part of the unsettled bays, harbors and creeks of the southern portion of the coast of Newfoundland before described, and of the coast of Labrador; the United States renouncing any liberty before enjoyed by their citizens to take fish within three marine miles of any coasts, bays, creeks or harbors of the British dominions in America not included within the above limits, *i. e.* Newfoundland and

Labrador. And 3dly. That American fishermen shall also be admitted to enter such bays or harbors for the purpose of shelter and of repairing damages therein, and also of purchasing wood and obtaining water, under such restrictions only as might be necessary to prevent their taking, drying or curing fish therein, or abusing the privileges reserved to them." Such are the stipulations of the treaty, and they are believed to be too plain and explicit to leave room for doubt or misapprehension, or render the discussion of the respective rights of the two countries at this time necessary. Indeed it does not appear that any conflicting questions of right between them have as yet arisen out of differences of opinion regarding the true intent and meaning of the treaty. It appears, however, that in the actual application of the provisions of the convention, (committed on the part of Great Britain to the hands of subordinate agents, subject to and controlled by local legislation,) difficulties, growing out of individual acts, have unfortunately sprung up from time to time, among the most important of which have been recent seizures of American vessels for supposed violations of the treaty. These have been made, it is believed, under color of a provincial law of 6 William IV., chapter 8, 1836, passed doubtless with a view to restrict vigorously, if not intended to aim a fatal blow at the fisheries of the United States on the coasts of Newfoundland.

It also appears, from information recently received by the government of the United States, that the provincial authorities assume a right to exclude the vessels of the United States from all their bays, (even including those of Fundy and Chaleurs,) and likewise to prohibit their approach within three miles of a line *drawn from headland to headland, instead of from the indents of the shores of the provinces.* They also assert the right of excluding them from British ports, unless in actual distress; warning them to depart, or get under weigh and leave harbor, whenever the provincial custom-house or British naval officer shall suppose that they have remained a reasonable time; and this without a full examination of the circumstances under which they may have entered the port. Now, the fishermen of the United States believe (and it would seem that they are right in their opinion, if uniform practice in any evidence of correct construction,) that they can with propriety take fish any where on the coasts of the British provinces, *if not nearer than three marine miles to land,* and have the right to resort to their ports for shelter, wood and water; nor has this claim, it is believed, ever been seriously disputed, based as it is on the plain and obvious terms of the convention. Indeed, the main object of the treaty was not only to secure to American fishermen, is the pursuit of their employment, the right of fishing, but likewise to insure to them as large a proportion of the conveniences afforded by the neighboring coasts of British settlements, as might be reconcilable with the just rights and interests of British subjects, and the due administration of her Majesty's dominions. The construction therefore, which has been attempted to be put upon the stipulations of the treaty by the authorities of Nova Scotia, is directly in conflict with their object, and entirely subversive of the rights and interests of the citizens of the United States. It is one moreover, which would lead to the abandonment, to a great extent, of a highly important branch of American industry, which could not for a moment be admitted by the government of the United States. The undersigned has also been instructed to acquaint Lord Palmerston that the American government has received information that in the House of Assembly of Nova Scotia during the session of 1839–'40, an address to her Majesty was voted, suggesting the extension to adjoining British colonies of rules and regulations relating to the fisheries, similar to those in actual operation in that province, and which have proved so onerous to the fishermen of the United States; and that efforts, it is understood, are still making to induce the other colonies to unite with Nova Scotia in this restrictive system. Some of the provisions of her code are of the most extraordinary character. Among these is one which declares that any foreign vessel *preparing* to fish within three miles of the coast of her Majesty's dominions in America shall, together with her cargo, be forfeited; that in all cases of seizure, the owner or claimant of the vessel, &c., shall be held to prove his innocence, or pay treble costs; that he shall be forced to try his action within three months, and give one month's notice at least to the seizing officer, containing everything intended to be proved against him, before any suit can be instistuted; and also prove that the notice has been given. The seizing officer, moreover, is almost wholly irresponsible, inasmuch as he is liable to no prosecution if the judge certifies that there was probable cause; and the plaintiff, if successful in his suit, is only to be entitled to *two pence damages without costs*, and the defendant fined *not more than one shilling*. In short, some of these rules and regulations are violations of well established principles of the common law of England, and of the principles of the just laws of all civilized nations, and would seem to have been designed to enable her Majesty's authorities to seize and confiscate with impunity American vessels, and embezzle indiscriminately the property of American citizens employed in the fisheries on the coasts of the British provinces.

It may be proper, also, on this occasion, to bring to the notice of her Majesty's government the assertion of the provincial legislature, "*that the Gut or Strait of Canso is a narrow strip of water, completely within and dividing several counties of the province*," and that the use of it by the vessels and citizens of the United States is in violation of the treaty of 1818. This strait separates Nova Scotia from the island of Cape Breton, which was not annexed to the province until the year 1820. Prior to that, in 1818, Cape Breton was enjoying a government of its own, entirely distinct from Nova Scotia, the strait forming the line of demarcation between them, and being then, as now, a thoroughfare for vessels passing into and out of the Gulf of St. Lawrence. The union of the two colonies cannot, therefore, be admitted as vesting in the province the right to close a passage which has been freely and indisputably used by the citizens of the United States since the year 1783. It is impossible, moreover, to conceive how the use on the part of the United States of this right of passage, common, it is believed to all other nations, can in any manner conflict with the letter or spirit of the existing treaty stipulations. The undersigned would therefore fain hope that her Majesty's government will be disposed to meet, as far as practicable, the wishes of the American government, in accomplishing in the fullest and most liberal manner the objects which both governments had in view in entering into the conventional arrangement of 1818.

He has accordingly been instructed to bring the whole subject under the consideration of her Majesty's government, and to remonstrate on the part of his government against the illegal and vexatious proceedings of the authorities of Nova Scotia against the citizens of the United States engaged in the fisheries, and to request that measures may be forthwith adopted by her Majesty's government to remedy the evils arising out of the misconstruction on the part of its provincial authorities of their conventional obligations, and prevent the possibility of the recurrence of similar acts.

The undersigned renews to Lord Palmerston assurances of his distinguished consideration.

A. STEVENSON.

[Enclosure.]

Lord Palmerston to Mr. Stevenson.

FOREIGN OFFICE, *April* 2, 1841.

The undersigned, her Majesty's principal Secretary of State for Foreign Affairs, has the honor to acknowledge the receipt of the note from Mr. Stevenson, Envoy Extraordinary and Minister Plenipotentiary from the United States of America, of the 27th ultimo, bringing under the notice of her Majesty's government certain proceedings of the colonial authorities of Nova Scotia in relation to the seizure and interruption of the vessels and citizens of the United States, engaged in intercourse with the ports of Nova Scotia, and the prosecution of the fisheries on its neighboring coasts; and the undersigned has lost no time in referring Mr. Stevenson's representation to the Secretary of State for the Colonial Department.

The undersigned has the honor to renew to Mr. Stevenson the assurances of his high consideration.

PALMERSTON.

[Extract.]

Mr. Stevenson to Mr. Webster.

LEGATION OF THE UNITED STATES,
London, May 18, 1841.

* * * * * * I also forward the copy of a second note from Lord Palmerston, relative to the fisheries and the intercourse of our vessels with Nova Scotia.

[Enclosure.]

Lord Palmerston to Mr. Stevenson.

FOREIGN OFFICE, *April* 28, 1841.

The undersigned, her Majesty's principal Secretary of State for Foreign Affairs, with reference to the note which he addressed to Mr. Stevenson, Envoy Extraordinary and Minister Plenipotentiary from the United States of America, dated the 2d instant, stating that he had referred to the Secretary of State for the Colonial Department, Mr. Stevenson's note of the

27th ultimo, respecting certain proceedings of the colonial authorities of Nova Scotia in relation to the seizure and interruption of the vessels and citizens of the United States of America engaged in intercourse with the ports of Nova Scotia, and in the prosecution of the fisheries on its neighboring coasts, has the honor to inform Mr. Stevenson, that he has since received from the Colonial Department a letter informing him that copies of the papers received from Mr. Stevenson would be forwarded to Lord Falkland, with instructions to inquire into the allegations contained therein, and to furnish a detailed report upon the subject.

The undersigned has the honor to renew to Mr. Stevenson the assurances of his high consideration.

PALMERSTON.

Mr. Upshur to Mr. Everett.

[No. 49.]

Department of State,
Washington, June 30, 1843.

Sir: I have the honor to transmit to you herewith, copies of a letter and accompanying papers relating to the seizure, on the 10th of May last, on the coast of Nova Scotia, by an officer of the provincial customs, of the American fishing schooner Washington, of Newburyport, Massachusetts, Cheny, master, for an alleged infraction of the stipulations of the convention of October 20, 1818, between the United States and Great Britain.

Upon a reference to the files of the legation at London, you will find that this complaint is not the first of a similar character which has arisen out of the proceedings of the authorities of Nova Scotia under their construction of the convention, and that representations upon the subject have heretofore been made to the British government on behalf of American citizens, but, so far as this department is advised, without leading to a satisfactory result.

For a full understanding of the whole question involved I would particularly point your attention to the instructions of this department to Mr. Stevenson, Nos. 71 and 89, of the respective dates of April 17, 1840, and February 20, 1841, and to the several despatches addressed by that minister to the Secretary of State, numbered 97, 99, 108, 120 and 124, during the years 1840 and 1841.

I need not remark upon the importance to the negotiating interests of the United States of having a proper construction put upon the first article of the convention of 1818 by the parties to it. That which has hitherto obtained is believed to be the correct one. The obvious necessity of an authoritative intervention to put an end to proceedings on the part of the British colonial authorities, alike conflicting with their conventional obligations and ruinous to the fortunes and subversive of the rights of an enterprising and deserving class of our fellow citizens, is too apparent to allow this government to doubt that the government of her Britannic Majesty will take efficient steps for the purpose. The President's confident expectation of an early and satisfactory adjustment of these difficulties is grounded upon his reliance on the sense of justice of the Queen's government, and on the fact that from the year 1818, the date of the convention, until some years after the enactment of the provincial law out of which these troubles have arisen, a *practical* construction has been given to the first article of that instrument which is firmly relied on as settling its meaning in favor of the rights of American citizens as claimed by the United States.

I have, therefore, to request that you will present this subject again to the consideration of her Majesty's government by addressing a note to the British Secretary of State for Foreign Affairs, reminding him that the letter of Mr. Stevenson to Lord Palmerston remains unanswered, and informing him of the anxious desire of the President that proper means should be taken to prevent the possibility of a recurrence of any like cause of complaint.

I am, sir, with great respect, your obedient servant,

A. P. UPSHUR.

EDWARD EVERETT, Esq., &c., &c., &c.

[Enclosure.]

BOSTON, *May* 23, 1843.

SIR: I transmit herewith a memorial of the owner of an American fishing vessel which has, within a few days past, been seized by the authorities of Nova Scotia for an alleged violation of treaty stipulations. I learn that many of the fishing vessels of this State would be liable to seizure under the construction which has been adopted by the British authorities in the present instance. The early attention of our government to the subject is therefore earnestly desired by those who are engaged in this branch of business, and more especially by the memorialists whose property is immediately in jeopardy.

I am, very respectfully, your obedient servant,

ROBERT C. WINTHROP.

Hon. H. S. LEGARE,
Secretary of State, &c., &c.

[Enclosure.]

BOSTON, *May* 17, 1843.

The undersigned, Charles Currier, of Newburyport, in the State of Massachusetts, respectfully represents that he is the owner of a schooner called the Washington, of and belonging to said Newburyport; on the 28th day of April last on a fishing cruise under the command of John C. Cheny as master, and manned by three seamen, of whom William Bragg, whose deposition accompanies this memorial, was one; that on the tenth day of the present month the said schooner, while her crew were engaged in taking fish at a *place ten miles distant from the coast of Nova Scotia*, was taken possession of by *an officer of the provincial customs* and taken into some port of the province of Nova Scotia, where she is still detained, and, as he has reason to apprehend, will be confiscated. The undersigned forwards herewith the deposition of the said Bragg, and begs leave to refer to the same for a more particular account of the case. As your memorialist believes that the master and crew of said vessel had not been guilty of violating any treaty or engagement between Great Britain and the United States, he humbly prays that the government of the United States will, as soon as may be, take effectual measures to restore to him his property so seized, with compensation for damages and expenses occasioned by such seizure.

CHARLES CURRIER.

To the Honorable HUGH S. LEGARE,
Acting Secretary of State for the United States.

[Enclosure.]

BOSTON, *May* 17, 1843.

I, William Bragg, of Seabrook, in the State of New Hampshire, on oath depose and say that, on the 28th day of April now last past, I sailed from Newburyport as a seaman in the schooner Washington, whereof John C. Cheney was master, said schooner bound upon a fishing excursion, there being four men all told on board said vessel, including the master; that the said master and crew fished from time to time between the coasts of Maine and Nova Scotia until the tenth day of the present month; that on the said last mentioned day, while engaged in taking fish at least ten miles from the coast of Nova Scotia, the said schooner was boarded by an officer employed in the British revenue service of the name of Darby, and taken possession of in the name of the British government, the said officer alleging that the place where we were fishing was within the bounds prohibited by treaty to American fishermen; that I, together with the other men belonging to the schooner, was then put on board a small vessel, and we were landed at a place near Digby; that the captain (Cheney) continued on board the schooner, whether voluntarily or not I do not know, and when we left the schooner the British officer was in command thereof, and set sail with her for Yarmouth, in said Nova Scotia, to which place I have no doubt the schooner was carried under his command; that on the 11th instant, I and the other men of the schooner got passage from Digby in a vessel bound for Portsmouth, New Hampshire, at which place we arrived on the 15th instant. I further depose and say, that at no time while I was on board said schooner did we or any of us take or attempt to take fish within *ten miles of the coast of Nova Scotia, New Brunswick,* or of the *islands belonging to either of those provinces;* that the place where said schooner was taken possession of, as aforesaid, was opposite to a place on the coasts of Nova Scotia called *Gulliver's-hole,* and is distant from Annapolis-gut about fifteen miles, the said Gulliver's-hole being to the southwestward of said Annapolis gut.

WILLIAM BRAGG.

UNITED STATES OF AMERICA, STATE OF MASSACHUSETTS, } *ss.*
County of Suffolk and City of Boston, }

On this 17th day of May, A. D. 1843, before me, John P. Bigelow, a notary public, duly constituted and sworn within and for said county and city, came the above William Bragg, and made oath that the statements by him above signed are true.

[L. S.] Witness my hand and notarial seal.

JOHN P. BIGELOW,
Notary Public.

[Extract.]

Mr. Everett to Mr. Upshur.

[No. 50.] LONDON, *August* 15, 1843.

*   *   *   *   *   *   *   *

Enclosed with this despatch will be found a note addressed by me to Lord Aberdeen, on the subject of the seizure of the fishing schooner Washington, on the coast of Nova Scotia.

I sent with it copies of the documents relative to this affair which accompanied your despatch No. 49.

[Enclosure.]

Mr. Everett to Lord Aberdeen.

46 GROSVENOR PLACE, *August* 10, 1843.

The undersigned, envoy extraordinary and minister plenipotentiary of the United States of America, has the honor to transmit to the earl of Aberdeen, her Majesty's principal Secretary of State for foreign affairs, the accompanying papers relating to the seizure on the 10th of May last, on the coast of Nova Scotia, by an officer of the provincial customs, of the American fishing schooner Washington, of Newburyport, in the State of Massachusetts, for an alleged infraction of the stipulations of the convention of the 20th of October, 1818, between the United States and Great Britain.

It appears from the deposition of William Bragg, a seaman on board the Washington, that at the time of her seizure she was not within ten miles of the coast of Nova Scotia. By the first article of the convention above alluded to, the United States renounce any liberty heretofore enjoyed or claimed by their inhabitants to take, dry, or cure fish on or within three marine miles of any of the coast of her Majesty's dominions in America, for which express provision is not made in the said article. This renunciation is the only limitation existing on the right of fishing upon the coasts of her Majesty's dominions in America, secured to the people of the United States by the third article of the treaty of 1783.

The right, therefore, of fishing on any part of the coast of Nova Scotia, at a greater distance than three miles, is so plain that it would be difficult to conceive on what ground it could be drawn in question, had not attempts been already made by the provincial authorities of her Majesty's colonies, to interfere with its exercise. These attempts have formed the subject of repeated complaints on the part of the government of the United States as will appear from several notes addressed by the predecessor of the undersigned to Lord Palmerston.

From the construction attempted to be placed, on former occasions, upon the first article of the treaty of 1818, by the colonial authorities, the undersigned supposes that the "Washington" was seized because she was found fishing in the Bay of Fundy, and on the ground that the lines within which American vessels are forbidden to fish, are to run from headland to headland, and not to follow the shore. It is plain, however, that neither the words nor the spirit of the convention admits of any such construction; nor, it is believed, was it set up by the provincial authorities for several years after the negotiation of that instrument. A glance at the map will show Lord Aberdeen that there is, perhaps, no part of the great extent of the seacoasts of her Majesty's possessions in America, in which the right of an American vessel to fish can be subject to less doubt than that in which the "Washington" was seized.

For a full statement of the nature of the complaints which have, from time to time, been made by the government of the United States against the proceedings of the colonial authorities of Great Britain, the undersigned invites the attention of Lord Aberdeen to a note of Mr. Stevenson, addressed to Lord Palmerston on the 27th March, 1841. The receipt of this note was acknowledged by Lord Palmerston on the 2d of April, and Mr. Stevenson was informed that the subject was referred by his lordship to the Secretary of State for the colonial department.

On the 28th of the same month Mr. Stevenson was further informed by Lord Palmerston, that he had received a letter from the colonial department, acquainting his lordship that Mr. Stevenson's communication would be forwarded to Lord Falkland with instructions to inquire into the allegations contained therein, and to furnish a detailed report upon the subject. The undersigned does not find on the files of this legation any further communication from Lord Palmerston in reply to Mr. Stevenson's letter of the 27th March, 1841, and he believes that letter still remains unanswered.

In reference to the case of the Washington and those of a similar nature which have formerly occurred, the undersigned cannot but remark upon the impropriety of the conduct of the colonial authorities in undertaking, without directions from her Majesty's government, to set up a new construction of a treaty between the United States and England, and in proceeding to act upon it by the forcible seizure of American vessels.

Such a summary procedure could only be justified by a case of extreme necessity, and where some grave and impending mischief required to be averted without delay. To proceed to the capture of vessels of a friendly power for taking a few fish within limits alleged to be forbidden, although allowed by the express terms of the treaty, must be regarded as a very objectionable stretch of provincial authority. The case is obviously one for the consideration of the two governments, and in which no disturbance of a right exercised without question for fifty years from the treaty of 1783, ought to be attempted by any subordinate authority. Even her Majesty's government, the undersigned is convinced, would not proceed in such a case to violent measures of suppression, without some understanding with the government of the United States, or, in the failure of an attempt to come to an understanding, without due notice given of the course intended to be pursued.

The undersigned need not urge upon Lord Aberdeen the desirableness of an authoritative intervention on the part of her Majesty's government to put an end to the proceedings conplained of. The President of the United States entertains a confidant expectation of an early and equitable adjustment of the difficulties which have been now for so long time under the consideration of her Majesty's government. This expectation is the result of the President's reliance upon the sense of justice of her Majesty's government, and of the fact, that, from the year 1818, the date of the convention, until some years after the attempts of the provincial authorities to restrict the rights of American vessels by colonial legislation, a *practical* construction was given to the first article of the convention, in accordance with the obvious purport of its terms and settling its meaning as understood by the United States.

The undersigned avails himself of this opportunity to tender to Lord Aberdeen the assurance of his distinguished consideration.

EDWARD EVERETT.

[Extract.]

Mr. Everett to Mr. Calhoun.

[No. 130.] LONDON, *May* 26, 1844.

SIR: In pursuance of instructions from the Department of State, I addressed a note to Lord Aberdeen on the 10th of August last, on the case of the Washington, a vessel belonging to the United States, and seized for having been found fishing within the Bay of Fundy. The receipt of my note was promptly acknowledged, and I was informed that it had been referred to the colonial department for inquiry. On the 15th ultimo the result of this inquiry was communicated to me in a note from Lord Aberdeen, which I herewith transmit to you, together with a copy of my reply, bearing date the 25th instant.

I have endeavored to present the strong points of our case in a favorable light; and I cannot doubt that the spirit and intent of the convention of 1818 are such as I have represented them to be in my answer to Lord Aberdeen. * * * * * * *

[Enclosure.]

Lord Aberdeen to Mr. Everett.

FOREIGN OFFICE, *April* 15, 1844.

The note which Mr. Everett, envoy extraordinary and minister plenipotentiary of the United States of America, addressed to the undersigned, her Majesty's principal secretary of state for foreign affairs, on the 10th of August last, respecting the seizure of the American fishing vessel Washington by the officers of Nova Scotia, having been duly referred to the colonial office, and by that office to the governor of Nova Scotia, the undersigned has now the honor to communicate to Mr. Everett the result of those references.

The complaint which Mr. Everett submits to her Majesty's government is that, contrary to the express stipulations of the convention concluded on the 20th of October, 1818, between Great Britain and the United States, an American fishing vessel was seized by the British authorities for fishing in the Bay of Fundy, where Mr. Everett affirms that, by the treaty, American vessels have a right to fish, provided they are at a greater distance than three marine miles from the coast.

Mr. Everett, in submitting this case, does not cite the words of the treaty, but states in general terms that, by the first article of said treaty the United States renounce any liberty heretofore enjoyed or claimed by their inhabitants to take, dry or cure fish on or within three miles of any of the coasts of her Majesty's dominions in America. Upon reference, however, to the words of the treaty, it will be seen that American vessels have no right to fish, and indeed are expressly debarred from fishing in any bay on the coast of Nova Scotia.

The words of the treaty of October, 1818, article 1, run thus: "And the United States hereby renounce forever any liberty heretofore enjoyed or claimed by the inhabitants thereof, to *take*, dry, or cure fish, on or *within three marine* miles of any of the coasts, *bays*, creeks or harbors of his Britannic Majesty's dominions in America, not included within the abovementioned limits, [that is, Newfoundland, Labrador, and other parts separate from Nova Scotia:] provided, however, that the American fishermen shall be *admitted to enter* such bays or harbors for the purpose of shelter," &c.

It is thus clearly provided that American fishermen shall not take fish within three marine miles of any bay of Nova Scotia, &c. If the treaty was intended to stipulate simply that American fishermen should not take fish within three miles of the coast of Nova Scotia, &c., there was no occasion for using the word "*bay*" at all. But the proviso at the end of the article shows that the word "bay" was used designedly; for it is expressly stated in that proviso, that under certain circumstances the American fishermen may enter *bays*, by which it is evidently meant that they may, under those circumstances, pass the sea-line which forms the entrance of the bay. The undersigned apprehends that this construction will be admitted by Mr. Everett.

That the Washington was found fishing within the Bay of Fundy is, the undersigned believes, an admitted fact, and she was seized accordingly.

The undersigned requests Mr. Everett to accept the assurances of his high consideration.

ABERDEEN.

EDWARD EVERETT, Esq.

[Enclosure.]

Mr. Everett to Mr. Aberdeen.

GROSVENOR PLACE, *May* 25, 1844.

The undersigned, Envoy Extraordinary and Minister Plenipotentiary of the United States of America, had the honor duly to receive the note of the 15th of April, addressed to him by the Earl of Aberdeen, her Majesty's principal Secretary of State for Foreign Affairs, in reply to the note of the undersigned of the 10th of August last, relative to the seizure of the American vessel, the Washington, for having been found fishing within the limits of the Bay of Fundy.

The note of the undersigned, of the 10th of August last, although its immediate occasion was the seizure of the Washington, contained a reference to the correspondence between Mr. Stevenson and Viscount Palmerston on the subject of former complaints of the American government, of the manner in which the fishing vessels of the United States had in several ways been interfered with by the provincial authorities, in contravention as is believed, of the treaty of October, 1818, between the two countries. Lord Aberdeen's attention was particularly invited to the fact that no answer as yet had been returned to Mr. Stevenson's note to Lord Palmerston, of 27th March, 1841, the receipt of which and its reference to the Colonial department were announced by a note of Lord Palmerston of the 2d April. The undersigned further observed that on the 28th of the same month Lord Palmerston acquainted Mr. Stevenson that his lordship had been advised from the Colonial office, that "copies of the papers received from Mr. Stevenson would be furnished to Lord Falkland, with instructions to inquire into the allegations contained therein, and to furnish a detailed report on the subject;" but that there was not found on the files of this legation any further communication from Lord Palmerston on the subject.

The note of Lord Aberdeen, of the 15th of April last, is confined exclusively to the case of the Washington; and it accordingly becomes the duty of the undersigned again to invite his lordship's attention to the correspondence above referred to between Mr. Stevenson aud Lord Palmerston, and to request that inquiry may be made, without unnecessary delay, into all the causes of complaint which have been made by the American government against the improper interference of the British colonial authorities with the fishing vessels of the United States.

In reference to the case of the Washington, Lord Aberdeen, in his note of the 15th of April, justifies her seizure by an armed provincial vessel, on the assumed fact that, as she was found fishing in the Bay of Fundy, she was within the limits from which the fishing vessels of the United States are excluded by the provisions of the convention between the two countries of October 1818.

The undersigned had remarked in his note of the 10th of August last, on the impropriety of the conduct of the colonial authorities in proceeding in reference to a question of construction of a treaty pending between the two countries, to decide the question in their own favor, and in virtue of that decision to order the capture of the vessels of a friendly State. A summary exercise of power of this kind, the undersigned is sure would never be resorted to by her Majesty's government, except in an extreme case, while a negotiation was in train on the point at issue. Such a procedure on the part of a local colonial authority, is of course highly objectionable, and the undersigned cannot but again invite the attention of Lord Aberdeen to this view of the subject.

With respect to the main question of the right of American vessels to fish within the acknowledged limits of the Bay of Fundy, it is necessary, for a clear understanding of the case, to go back to the treaty of 1783.

By this treaty it was provided that the citizens of the United States should be allowed "to take fish of every kind on such part of the coast of

Newfoundland as British fishermen shall use, (but not to dry or cure the same on that island) and also on the coasts, bays and creeks of all other of his Britannic Majesty's dominions in America, and that the American fishermen shall have liberty to dry and cure fish in any of the unsettled bays, harbors and creeks of Nova Scotia, Magdalen islands and Labrador, so long as the same shall remain unsettled; but so soon as the same or either of them shall be settled, it shall not be lawful for the said fishermen to dry or cure fish at such settlement without a previous agreement for that purpose with the inhabitants, proprietors or possessors of that ground."

These privileges and conditions were in reference to a country of which a considerable portion was then unsettled, likely to be attended with differences of opinion as to what should, in the progress of time, be accounted a settlement from which American fishermen might be excluded. These differences in fact arose, and by the year 1818 the state of things was so far changed that her Majesty's government thought it necessary in negotiating the convention of that year, entirely to except the province of Nova Scotia from the number of the places which might be frequented by Americans as being in part unsettled, and to provide that the fishermen of the United States should not pursue their occupation within three miles of the shores, bays, creeks and harbors of that and other parts of her Majesty's possessions similarly situated. The privilege reserved to American fishermen by the treaty of 1783, of taking fish in all the waters and drying them on all the unsettled portions of the coast of these possessions was accordingly by the convention of 1818 restricted as follows:

"The United States hereby renounce forever any liberty heretofore enjoyed or claimed by the inhabitants thereof, to take, dry, or cure fish on or within three marine miles of any of the coasts, bays, creeks or harbors of his Britannic Majesty's dominions in America, not included within the above mentioned limits; provided, however, that the American fishermen shall be admitted to enter such bays or harbors for the purpose of sheltering and repairing damages therein, of purchasing wood, and of obtaining water, and for no other purpose whatever."

The existing doubt as to the construction of the provision arises from the fact that a broad arm of the sea runs up to the northeast, between the provinces of New Brunswick and Nova Scotia. This arm of the sea being commonly called the Bay of Fundy, though not in reality possessing all the characters usually implied by the term "bay," has of late years been claimed by the provincial authorities of Nova Scotia to be included among "the coasts, bays, creeks and harbors forbidden to American fishermen.

An examination of the map is sufficient to show the doubtful nature of this construction. It was notoriously the object of the article of the treaty in question to put an end to the difficulties which had grown out of the operations of the fishermen from the United States along the coasts and upon the shores of the settled portions of the country, and for that purpose to remove their vessels to a distance not exceeding three miles from the same. In estimating this distance, the undersigned admits it to be the intent of the treaty, as it is itself reasonable, to have regard to the general line of the coast; and to consider its bays, creeks and harbors, that is, the indentations usually so accounted, as included within that line. But the undersigned cannot admit it to be reasonable, instead of thus following the general directions of the coast, to draw a line from the southwestern-most point of Nova Scotia to the termination of the northeastern boundary between the United States and New Brunswick, and to consider the arms of the sea which will thus be cut off, and which cannot, on that line be less than sixty miles wide, as one of the bays on the coast from which American vessels are excluded. By this interpretation the fishermen of the United States would be shut out from the waters distant, not three, but thirty miles from any part of the colonial coast. The undersigned cannot perceive that any assignable object of the restriction imposed by the convention of 1818 on the fishing privilege accorded to the citizens of the United States by the treaty of 1783 requires such a latitude of construction.

It is obvious that (by the terms of the treaty) the furthest distance to which fishing vessels of the United States are obliged to hold themselves from the colonial coasts and bays, is three miles. But, owing to the peculiar configuration of these coasts, there is a succession of bays indenting the shores both of New Brunswick and Nova Scotia, within the Bay of Fundy. The vessels of the United States have a general right to approach all the bays in her Majesty's colonial dominions, within any distance not less than three miles—a privilege from the enjoyment of which they will be wholly excluded—in this part of the coast, if the broad arm of the sea which flows up between New Brunswick and Nova Scotia, is itself to be considered one of the forbidden bays.

Lastly—and this consideration seems to put the matter beyond doubt—the construction set up by her Majesty's colonial authorites, would altogether nullify another, and that a most important stipulation of the treaty, about which there is no controversy, viz: the privilege reserved to American fishing vessels of taking shelter and repairing damages in the bays within which they are forbidden to fish. There is, of course, no shelter nor means of repairing damages for a vessel entering the Bay of Fundy, in itself considered. It is necessary, before relief or succor of any kind can be had, to traverse that broad arm of the sea and reach the bays and harbors, properly so called, which indent the coast, and which are no doubt the bays and harbors referred to in the convention of 1818. The privilege of entering the latter in extremity of weather, reserved by the treaty, is of the utmost importance. It enables the fisherman, whose equipage is always very slender (that of the Washington was four men all told) to pursue his laborious occupation with comparative safety, in the assurance that in one of the sudden and dangerous changes of weather so frequent and so terrible on this iron bound coast, he can take shelter in a *neighboring* and friendly port. To forbid him to approach within thirty miles of that port, except for shelter in extremity of weather, is to forbid him to resort there for that purpose. It is keeping him at such a distance at sea as wholly to destroy the value of the privilege expressly reserved.

In fact it would follow, if the construction contended for by the British colonial authorities were sustained, that two entirely different limitations would exist in reference to the right of shelter reserved to American vessels on the shores of her Majesty's colonial possessions. They would be allowed to fish within three miles of the place of shelter along the greater part of the coast; while in reference to the entire extent of shore within the Bay of Fundy, they would be wholly prohibited from fishing along the coast, and would be kept at a distance of twenty or thirty miles from any place of refuge in case of extremity. There are certainly no obvious principles which render such a construction probable.

The undersigned flatters himself that these considerations will go far to satisfy Lord Aberdeen of the correctness of the American understanding of the words "Bay of Fundy," arguing on the terms of the treaties of 1783 and 1818. When it is admitted that, as the undersigned is advised, there has been no attempt till late years to give them any other construction than that for which the American government now contends, the point would seem to be placed beyond doubt.

Meantime Lord Aberdeen will allow that this is a question, however doubtful, to be settled exclusively by her Majesty's government and that of the United States. No disposition has been evinced by the latter to anticipate the decision of the question; and the undersigned must again represent it to the Earl of Aberdeen as a matter of just complaint and surprise on the part of his government, that the opposite course has been pursued by her Majesty's colonial authorities, who have proceeded (the undersigned is confident without instructions from London,) to capture and detain an American vessel on a construction of the treaty which is a matter of discussion between the two governments, and while the undersigned is actually awaiting a communication on the subject promised to his predecessor.

This course of conduct, it may be added, objectionable under any circumstances, finds no excuse in any supposed urgency of the case. The Washington was not within three times the limit admitted to be prescribed in reference to the approach of American vessels to all other parts of the coast, and in taking a few fish, out of the abundance which exists in those seas, she certainly was inflicting no injury on the interests of the colonial population which required this summary and violent measure of redress.

The undersigned trusts that the Earl of Aberdeen, on giving a renewed consideration to the case, will order the restoration of the Washington, if still detained, and direct the colonial authorities to abstain from the further capture of the fishing vessels of the United States under similar circumstances, till it has been decided between the two governments whether the Bay of Fundy is included among "the coasts, bays, creeks and harbors" which American vessels are not permitted to approach within three miles.

The undersigned requests Lord Aberdeen to accept the assurances of his distinguished consideration.

EDWARD EVERETT.

The Earl of Aberdeen, &c., &c.

[Extract.]

Mr. Calhoun to Mr. Everett.

[No. 97.] Department of State,
Washington, July 5, 1844.

Sir: I have the honor to acknowedge the receipt of your despatches to No. 147, inclusive.

The President is perfectly satisfied with the manner in which you have presented the case of the American vessel Washington, seized by British colonial authorities for having been found fishing within the Bay of Fundy, and with the argument on the main question contained in your note to the Earl of Aberdeen of the 25th of May last, involving the interpretation to be given to the provisions of the convention of 1818. * * * * * *

Mr. Calhoun to Mr. Everett.

[No. 105.] DEPARTMENT OF STATE,
Washington, September 6, 1844.

SIR: It would seem from a perusal of the papers which accompany this despatch that an outrage has recently been committed by the British cutter Sylph on the American fishing schooner Argus, William Doughty master, off the coast of Cape Breton, much in character with some of those which have from time to time been made the subject of remonstrance by this government. Instructions in cases analagous to the one now under consideration having already been given by this department to the legation of the United States at London, it is not deemed necessary to repeat them at this time for the purpose of expressing the views of this government, or of pointing out the course which you will be expected to pursue in presenting the case of the Argus to the notice of the British government.

I am, sir, respectfully, your obedient servant,

J. C. CALHOUN.

EDWARD EVERETT, Esq.

List of accompanying papers.

J. and J. Starling to the Secretary of State, (one enclosure) dated 26th August, 1844.

United States Consul at Halifax to Messrs. J. and J. Starling, 19th August, 1844.

Deposition of Edwin Doughty.

Deposition of Joshua Doughty.

[Enclosure.]

PORTLAND, *August* 26, 1844.

SIR: We beg leave to lay before you the enclosed letter from our consul at Halifax, and earnestly beg for your interference to seej ustice done to us. We are fishermen and have but little property and are wholly unable to pay the sum the consul says is required by the court to be secured before we are permitted to have a trial of our vessel. Our vessel was fifteen miles from any land when she was seized, and if the British construction of the treaty is right, then no American can fish in the Bay of Fundy, even if he is fifty miles from any shore.

As well might we draw a line from Cape Florida to Cape Cod and say that *meant* three "marine miles from the shore" between these capes.

It appears, from the consul's letter, to be the determination of the English government to condemn the vessel, and all our vessels found within "three marine miles" of a line drawn from cape to cape. Our vessel had two hundred and fifty quintals of fish on board, and the vessel was valuable to us and to her crew, who were turned on shore without funds or means to help them home. It appears that this seizure is made to settle the disputed construction of the treaty, and we most confidently rely on the strong arm of our government to defend and protect us in our honestly acquired property and peaceful industry.

With great respect, we are, sir, your most obedient servants,

J. & J. STARLING.

To the Hon. J. C. CALHOUN,
Secretary of State, Washington City.

[Enclosure.]

I, Edwin Doughty, of Portland, State of Maine, aged twenty-three years, on oath testify and say, that I was shipped in April last as salter on board the fishing schooner Argus, of Portland, of which vessel William Doughty was master or skipper; that we sailed in April for Cape Sables, made our freight of fish and returned about the 10th of June last; we sailed again about the 18th of June, and in six days arrived on St. Ann's bank, which lies between Cow-bay head and Cape North, and is more than fifteen marine miles from any land; we fished there until the sixth day of July, when we were captured by a cutter called the Sylph, of Halifax, being a Nova Scotia government schooner commanded by a man named Dodge, and carried us into Sidney. We arrived at Sidney about five o'clock in the morning of the 7th July, where we lay until ten o'clock next morning when Dodge ordered us all to leave the Argus, in fifteen minutes, and that all of our wearing apparal that we did not get out in fifteen minutes Dodge declared would be held with the prize. We all left within the fifteen minutes, but some of the crew forgot some of their effects and requested leave to go on board for them; this request was denied, nor would this Dodge deliver them up. We told this Dodge that we had not a cent of money, and requested leave to take some of our bread, beef and pork on shore to live on for a day or two until we could find some chance to get home. He replied we should not have a single biscuit; we urged our destitute situation, but all the reply we got was that our situation was nothing to him. When Dodge took us our skipper told him we were more than fifteen miles from land; this Dodge admitted, for from where we lay Cape North bore north by compass, and Cow-head bore SSW. by compass, and on inspection the chart will show we were more than sixteen miles from any shore, and in fact we were all of three miles outside of a line drawn from Cow-bay head to Cape North; but Dodge said we were within three miles of such a line, and on their construction of the treaty that we were a lawful prize; he said he seized us to settle the question. Dodge read the annexed document as his authority and gave it to my father, the skipper, who gave it to me to bring home to the owners.

I got on board the fishing schooner Emma, of Portland, and came home with two of my brothers, and left my father and two of the crew at Sidney who were to go to Halifax.

EDWARD DOUGHTY.

CUMBERLAND, MAINE, *August* 26, 1844.

Then the above mentioned Edward Doughty personally appeared and made solemn oath to the foregoing deposition by him subscribed before me.

JOHN ANDERSON,
Justice of the Peace.

I, Joshua Doughty, of Portland, in the county of Cumberland and State of Maine, aged fourteen years, on oath declare that I was a boy on board the fishing schooner Argus, shipped in April last, and was in her until she was captured by the British cutter Sylph on the ninth of July last. I further say that I was present at the noting of the deposition of my brother, Edward Doughty, and that all he has related of our capture and treatment is true.

his
JOSHUA × DOUGHTY.
mark.

Witness: JOHN ANDERSON.

Cumberland, ss: *August* 26, 1844.

Then the above named Joshua Doughty personally appeared and made oath to the foregoing deposition by him subscribed before me.

JOHN ANDERSON,
Justice of the Peace.

[Enclosure.]

CONSULATE OF THE UNITED STATES,
Halifax, Nova Scotia, August 19, 1844.

GENTLEMEN: I have to inform you that William Doughty, master of schooner "Argus," called at my office on the 17th instant, and stated that his vessel had been seized by one of the colonial cruizers off the Cape Breton coast on the 6th of this month, and was taken into Sidney for an infraction on the British fisheries; or rather from the construction put upon the treaty of 1818 by the crown officers in England, which states that the "three marine miles" shall be from *headlands*. The seizing officer has determined to prosecute the suit, as the attorney general this day informed me; it will be two months ere the admiralty court will be convened. I have endeavored thus far to procure the release of this vessel, but without effect. The expenses in the court are very heavy, and previous to defending a suit, the judge requires security to the amount of three hundred dollars, so that generally speaking it is better to let the suit go by default, and purchase the vessel after condemnation. The master of the Argus and two of the crew are here, waiting a passage to Boston; as they have no means you will please establish a credit with Alfred Greenough, esq., Boston, for my account, say to the amount of fifty dollars, or authorize him to pay the masters bill for the amount of his expenses here and passage to Boston. I hold the depositions of Captain Doughty and two of his crew.

With respect,

T. B. LIVINGSTON,
United States Consul.

Messrs. J. & J. STARLING, *Portland.*

[Extract.]

Mr. Everett to Mr. Calhoun.

[No. 187.] LONDON, *October* 9, 1844.

SIR: Your instructions No. 105, dated September 6, and enclosing sundry papers relative to the seizure of the American fishing vessel the "Argus," by a Nova Scotia govenment schooner, were received by me a short time since.

I transmit herewith a copy of a note which I have addressed to Lord Aberdeen on the subject.

* * * * * * * *

Having discussed the general principles involved in the question in my note to Lord Aberdeen, of the 26th of May last, in a manner which the President has been pleased to approve, I have thought it unnecessary to go over the ground again on this occasion. * * *

JOHN C. CALHOUN, Esq.,
Secretary of State.

[Enclosure.]

GROSVENOR PLACE, *October* 9, 1844.

The undersigned, envoy extraordinary and minister plenipotentiary of the United States of America, has the honor to transmit to the Earl of Aberdeen, her Majesty's principal Secretary of State for foreign affairs, the accompanying papers relating to the capture of an American fishing vessel the "Argus," by a government cutter from Halifax, the "Sylph," on the 6th of July last.

In addition to the seizure of the vessel, her late commander, as Lord Aberdeen will perceive from his deposition, complains of harsh treatment on the part of the captors.

The grounds assigned for the capture of this vessel are not stated with great distinctness. They appear to be connected partly by the construction set up by her Majesty's provincial authorities in America, that the line within which vessels of the United States are forbidden to fish, is to be drawn from headland to headland, and not to follow the indentations of the coast, and partly with the regulations established by those authorities, in consequence of the annexation of Cape Breton to Nova Scotia.

With respect to the former point, the undersigned deems it unnecessary, on this occasion, to add anything to the observations contained in his note to Lord Aberdeen, of the 25th of May, on the subject of limitations of the right secured to American fishing vessels by the treaty of 1783 and the convention of 1818, in reply to the note of his lordship of the 15th of April on the same subject. As far as the capture of the Argus was made under the authority of the act annexing Cape Breton to Nova Scotia, the undersigned would observe that he is under the impression that the question of the legality of that measure is still pending before the judicial committee of her Majesty's privy council. It would be very doubtful whether rights secured to American vessels under public compacts could, under any circumstances, be impaired by acts of subsequent domestic legislation; but to proceed to capture American vessels, in virtue of such acts, while their legality is drawn in question by the home government, seems to be a measure as unjust as it is harsh.

Without enlarging on these views of the subject, the undersigned would invite the attention of the Earl of Aberdeen to the severity and injustice which in other respects characterize the laws and regulations adopted by her majesty's provincial authorities against the fishing vessels of the United States. Some of the provisions of the provincial law, in reference to the seizures which it authorizes of American vessels, were pronounced, in a note of Mr. Stephenson to Viscount Palmerston of the 27th of March, 1841, to be "violations of well-established principles of the common law of England, and of the principles of the just laws of well civilized nations;" and this strong language was used by Mr. Stevenson under the express instructions of his government.

A demand of security to defend the suit from persons so little able to furnish it as the captains of small fishing schooners, and so heavy that, in the language of the Consul at Halifax, "it is generally better to let the suit go by default," must be regarded as a provision of this description. Others still more oppressive are pointed out in Mr. Stevenson's note above referred to, in reference to which the undersigned finds himself obliged to repeat the remark made in his note to Lord Aberdeen of the 10th of August, 1843, that he believes it still remains unanswered.

It is stated by the captain of the "Argus" that the commander of the Nova Scotia schooner by which he was captured said that he was within three miles of the line beyond which, "on their construction of the treaty, we were a lawful prize, and that he seized us to settle the question."

The undersigned again feels it his duty, on behalf of his government, formally to protest against an act of this description. American vessels of trifling size, and pursuing a branch of industry of the most harmless description which, however beneficial to themselves, occasions no detriment to others, instead of being turned off the debatable fishing ground—a remedy fully adequate to the alleged evil—are proceeded against as if engaged in the most undoubted infractions of municipal law or the law of nations; captured and sent into port, their crews deprived of their clothing and personal effects, and the vessels subjected to a mode of procedure in the courts which amounts in many cases to confiscation; and this is done to settle the construction of a treaty.

A course so violent and unnecessarily harsh would be regarded by any government as a just cause of complaint against any other with whom it might differ in the construction of a national compact. But when it is considered that these are the acts of a provincial government, with whom that of the United States has and can have no intercourse, and that they continue and are repeated while the United States and Great Britain, the only parties to the treaty the purport of whose provisions is called in question, are amicably discussing the matter, with every wish, on both sides, to bring it to a reasonable settlement, Lord Aberdeen will perceive that it becomes a subject of complaint of the most serious kind.

As such, the undersigned is instructed again to bring it to Lord Aberdeen's notice, and to express the confident hope that such measures of redress as the urgency of the case requires will, at the instance of his lordship, be promptly resorted to.

The undersigned avails himself of this opportunity to renew to the Earl of Aberdeen the assurance of his distinguished consideration.

EDWARD EVERETT.

The Earl of Aberdeen, &c., &c., &c.

Mr. Everett to Mr. Calhoun.

[No. 204.] London, *November* 4, 1844.

Sir: With my despatch No. 187, of the 9th of October, I transmitted a copy of a note of the same date, addressed by me to Lord Aberdeen, on the subject of an American fishing vessel, the Argus, captured off the coast of Cape Breton by a provincial cruiser.

I received on the 19th inst, and of course too late for transmission by the Halifax steamer, which sailed that day from Liverpool, the accompanying note from Lord Aberdeen, informing me that my communication had been referred to the Colonial Department for investigation, and that I should hear again from him as soon as the result of the inquiry should be made known to him.

I am, sir, with great respect, your obedient servant,

EDWARD EVERETT.

John C. Calhoun, Esq.,
Secretary of State.

[Enclosure.]

Lord Aberdeen to Mr. Everett.

Foreign Office, *October* 12, 1844.

The undersigned, her Majesty's Principal Secretary of State for Foreign Affairs, has the honor to acknowledge the receipt of the note dated the 9th instant, from Mr. Everett, Envoy Extraordinary and Minister Plenipotentiary of the United States of America, bringing forward the complaint of the master of the American schooner Argus against the seizure of his vessel off the Cape Breton coast by one of her Majesty's colonial cruisers.

The undersigned has lost no time in referring Mr. Everett's letter to her Majesty's Principal Secretary of State for the colonies, with a request that an inquiry may be instituted into this affair; and the undersigned will again have the honor of communicating with Mr. Everett upon this subject as soon as the result of the inquiry shall have been made known to the undersigned.

The undersigned avails himself of this opportunity to renew to Mr. Everett the assurance of his high consideration.

ABERDEEN.

Edward Everett, Esq.

[Extracts.]

Mr. Everett to Mr. Calhoun.

[No. 278.] London, *March* 25, 1845.

Sir: You are aware that the construction of the first article of the convention between Great Britain and the United States, of 1818, relative to the right of fishing in the waters of the Anglo-American dependencies, has long been in discussion between the two governments. Instructions on this subject were several times addressed by Mr. Forsyth to my predecessor, particularly in a despatch of the 20th of February, 1841, which formed the basis of an able and elaborate note from Mr. Stevenson to Lord Palmerston, of the 27th of the following month. Mr. Stevenson's representations were acknowledged, and referred by the Colonial Office to the provincial government of Nova Scotia; but no other answer was returned to them.

The exclusion of American fishermen from the waters of the Bay of Fundy was the most prominent of the grievances complained of on behalf of the United States. Having received instructions from the department in reference to the seizure of the "Washington" of Newburyport, for fishing in the Bay of Fundy, I represented the case to Lord Aberdeen in a note of the 10th of August, 1843. An answer was received to this note on the 15th of April following, in which Lord Aberdeen confined himself to stating that by the terms of the convention the citizens of the United States were not allowed to fish within three miles of any bay upon the coast of the British American colonies, and could not, therefore, be permitted to pursue their avocation within the Bay of Fundy. I replied to this note on the 25th of May following, and endeavored to show that it was the spirit and design of the first article of the convention of 1818 to reserve to the people of the United States the right of fishing within three miles of the coast. Some remarks on the state of the controversy at that time will be found in my despatch, No. 130, of the 26th of May last.

On the 9th of October last, in obedience to your instructions, No. 105, I addressed a note to Lord Aberdeen in reference to the case of the "Argus" of Portland, which was captured while fishing on St. Anne's bank, off the northeastern coast of Cape Breton. The papers relative to this case left the precise grounds of the seizure of the "Argus" in some uncertainty. It was, however, sufficiently apparent that they were, to some extent at least, similar to those for which the "Washington" had been captured.

I received a few days since, and herewith transmit a note from Lord Aberdeen, containing the satisfactory intelligence that after a reconsideration of the subject, although the Queen's government adhere to the construction of the convention which they have always maintained, they have still come to the determination of relaxing from it, so far as to allow American fishermen to pursue their avocations in the Bay of Fundy.

* * * * * * * * * * *

I thought it proper, in replying to Lord Aberdeen's note, to recognise in ample terms the liberal spirit evinced by her Majesty's government, in relaxing from what they consider their right. At the same time I felt myself bound to say that the United States could not accept as a mere favor what they had always claimed as a matter of right, secured by the treaty.

Lord Aberdeen to Mr. Everett.

Foreign Office, *March* 10, 1845.

The undersigned, her Majesty's principal Secretary of State for Foreign Affairs, duly referred to the Colonial Department the note which Mr. Everett, Envoy Extraordinary and Minister Plenipotentiary of the United States of America, did him the honor to address to him on the 25th of May last, respecting the case of the "Washington," fishing vessel, and on the general question of the right of United States fishermen to pursue their calling in the Bay of Fundy; and having shortly since received the answer of that department, the undersigned is now enabled to make a reply to Mr. Everett's communication, which he trusts will be found satisfactory.

In acquitting himself of this duty, the undersigned will not think it necessary to enter into a lengthened argument in reply to the observations which have at different times been submitted to her Majesty's government by Mr. Stevenson and Mr. Everett, on the subject of the right of fishing in the Bay of Fundy, as claimed in behalf of the United States' citizens. The undersigned will confine himself to stating that after the most deliberate reconsideration of the subject, and with every desire to do full justice to the United States, and to view the claims put forward on behalf of United States' citizens in the most favorable light, her Majesty's government are nevertheless still constrained to deny the right of United States' citizens, under the treaty of 1818, to fish in that part of the Bay of Fundy which, from its geographical position, may properly be considered as included within the British possessions.

Her Majesty's government must still maintain, and in this view they are fortified by high legal authority, that the Bay of Fundy is rightfully claimed by Great Britain as a bay within the meaning of the treaty of 1818. And they equally maintain the position which was laid down in the note of the undersigned, dated the 15th of April last, that, with regard to the other bays on the British American coasts, no United States' fisherman has, under that convention, the right to fish within three miles of the *entrance* of such bays as designated by a line drawn from headland to headland at that entrance.

But while her Majesty's government still feel themselves bound to maintain these positions as a matter of right, they are nevertheless not insensible to the advantages which would accrue to both countries from a relaxation of the exercise of that right; to the United States as conferring a material benefit on their fishing trade; and to Great Britain and the United States, conjointly and equally, by the removal of a fertile source of disagreement between them.

Her Majesty's government are also anxious, at the same time that they uphold the just claims of the British crown, to evince by every reasonable concesssion their desire to act liberally and amicably towards the United States.

The undersigned has accordingly much pleasure in announcing to Mr. Everett, the determination to which her Majesty's government have come to relax in favor of the United States fishermen, that right which Great Britain has hitherto exercised, of excluding those fishermen from the British portion of the Bay of Fundy, and they are prepared to direct their colonial authorities to allow henceforward the United States fishermen to pursue their avocations in any part of the Bay of Fundy, provided they do not approach, except in the cases specified in the treaty of 1818, within three miles of the *entrance* of any bay on the coast of Nova Scotia or New Brunswick.

In thus communicating to Mr. Everett the liberal intentions of her Majesty's government, the undersigned desires to call Mr. Everett's attention to the fact that the produce of the labor of the British colonial fishermen is at the present moment excluded by prohibitory duties on the part of the United States from the markets of that country; and the undersigned would submit to Mr. Everett that the moment at which the British government are making a liberal concession to United States' trade, might well be deemed favorable for a counter concession on the part of the United States to British trade, by the reduction of the duties which operate so prejudicially to the interests of the British colonial fishermen.

The undersigned has the honor to renew to Mr. Everett, the assurances of his high consideration.

ABERDEEN.

[Enclosure.]

Mr. Everett to Lord Aberdeen.

GROSVENOR PLACE, *March* 25, 1845.

The undersigned, envoy extraordinary and minister plenipotentiary of the United States of America, has the honor to acknowledge the receipt of a note of the 10th instant from the Earl of Aberdeen, her Majesty's principal Secretary of State for foreign affairs, in reply to the communication of the undersigned of the 15th of May last, on the case of the "Washington," and the construction given by the government of the United States to the convention of 1818, relative to the right of fishing on the coasts of Nova Scotia and New Brunswick.

Lord Aberdeen acquaints the undersigned, that, after the most deliberate reconsideration of the subject, and with every desire to do full justice to the United States and to view the claims put forward on behalf of their citizens in the most favorable light, her Majesty's government are nevertheless still constrained to deny the right of citizens of the United States, under the treaty of 1818, to fish in that part of the Bay of Fundy which from its geographical position may properly be considered as included within the British possessions; and also to maintain that, with regard to the other bays on the British American coasts, no United States fisherman has, under that convention, the right to fish within three miles of the *entrance* of such bay, as designated by a line drawn from headland to headland at that entrance.

Lord Aberdeen, however, informs the undersigned that, although continuing to maintain these positions as a matter of right, her Majesty's government are not insensible to the advantages which might accrue to both countries from a relaxation in its exercise; that they are anxious, while upholding the just claims of the British crown, to evince by every reasonable concession their desire to act liberally and amicably towards the United States; and that her Majesty's government have accordingly come to the determination "to relax in favor of the United States fishermen the right which Great Britain has hitherto exercised of excluding those fishermen from the British portion of the Bay of Fundy, and are prepared to direct their colonial authorities to allow, henceforward, the United States fishermen to pursue their avocations in any part of the Bay of Fundy, provided they do not approach, except in the cases specified in the treaty of 1818, within three miles of the entrance of any bay on the coast of Nova Scotia or New Brunswick."

The undersigned receives with great satisfaction this communication from Lord Aberdeen, which promises the permanent removal of a fruitful cause of disagreement between the two countries, in reference to a valuable portion of the fisheries in question. The government of the United States, the undersigned is persuaded, will duly appreciate the friendly motives which have led to the determination on the part of her Majesty's government announced in Lord Aberdeen's note, and which he doubts not will have the natural effect of acts of liberality between powerful states, of producing benefits to both parties, beyond any immediate interest which may be favorably affected.

While he desires, however, without reserve, to express his sense of the amicable disposition evinced by her Majesty's government on this occasion in relaxing in favor of the United States the exercise of what, after deliberate reconsideration, fortified by high legal authority, is deemed an unquestioned right of her Majesty's government, the undersigned would be unfaithful to his duty did he omit to remark to Lord Aberdeen that no arguments have at any time been adduced to shake the confidence of the government of the United States in their own construction of the treaty. While they have ever been prepared to admit, that in the letter of one expression of that instrument there is some reason for claiming a right to exclude United States fishermen from the Bay of Fundy, (it being difficult to deny to that arm of the sea the name of "bay," which long geographical usage has assigned to it,) they have ever strenuously maintained that it is only on their own construction of the entire article that its known design in reference to the regulation of the fisheries admits of being carried into effect.

The undersigned does not make this observation for the sake of detracting from the liberality evinced by her Majesty's government in relaxing from what they regard as their right; but it would be placing his own government in a false position to accept as mere favor that for which they have so long and strenuously contended as due to them under the convention.

It becomes the more necessary to make this observation, in consequence of some doubt as to the extent of the proposed relaxation. Lord Aberdeen, after stating that her Majesty's government felt themselves constrained to adhere to the right of excluding the United States fishermen from the Bay of Fundy, and also with regard to other bays on the British American coasts, to maintain the position that no United States fisherman has, under that convention, the right to fish within three miles of the *entrance* of such bays, as designated by a line drawn from headland to headland at that entrance, adds, that "while her Majesty's government still feel themselves bound to maintain these positions as a matter of right, they are not insensible to the advantages which would accrue to both countries from the relaxation of that right."

This form of expression might seem to indicate that the relaxation proposed had reference to both positions; but when Lord Aberdeen proceeds to state more particularly its nature and extent, he confines it to a permission to be granted to "the United States fishermen to pursue their avocations in any part of the Bay of Fundy, provided they do not approach except in the cases specified in the treaty of 1818, within three miles of the *entrance* of any bay on the coast of Nova Scotia and New Brunswick," which entrance is defined, in another part of Lord Aberdeen's note, as being designated by a line drawn from headland to headland.

In the case of the "Washington," which formed the subject of the note of the undersigned of the 25th May, 1844, to which the present communication of Lord Aberdeen is a reply, the capture complained of was in the waters of the Bay of Fundy; the principal portion of the argument of the undersigned was addressed to that part of the subject; and he is certainly under the impression that it is the point of greatest interest in the discussions which have been hitherto carried on between the two governments, in reference to the United States' right of fishery on the Anglo-American coasts.

In the case, however, of the "Argus," which was treated in the note of the undersigned of the 9th of October, the capture was in the waters which wash the north-eastern coast of Cape Breton, a portion of the Atlantic ocean intercepted indeed between a straight line drawn from Cape North to the northern head of Cow bay, but possessing none of the characters of a bay, (far less so than the Bay of Fundy,) and not called a "bay" on any map which the undersigned has seen. The aforesaid line is a degree of latitude in length; and as far as reliance can be placed on the only maps (English ones) in the possession of the undersigned on which this coast is distinctly laid down, it would exclude vessels from fishing grounds which might be thirty miles from the shore.

Lord Aberdeen, in his note of the 10th instant, on the case of the "Argus," observes that, "as the point of the construction of the convention of 1818, in reference to the right of fishing in the Anglo-American dependencies by citizens of the United States, is treated in another note of the undersigned of this date, relative to the case of the "Washington," the undersigned abstains from again touching on that subject."

This expression taken by itself would seem to authorize the expectation that the waters where these two vessels respectively were captured would be held subject to the same principles, whether of restriction or relaxation, as indeed all the considerations which occur to the undersigned as having probably led her Majesty's government to the relaxation in reference to the Bay of Fundy, exist in full and even superior force in reference to the waters on the north-eastern coast of Cape Breton, where the "Argus" was seized. But if her Majesty's provincial authorities are permitted to regard as a "bay" any portion of the sea which can be cut off by a direct line connecting two points of the coast, however destitute in other respects of the character usually implied by that name, not only will the waters on the north-eastern coast of Cape Breton, but on many other parts of the shores of the Anglo-American dependencies where such exclusion has not yet been thought of, be prohibited to American fishermen. In fact, the waters which wash the entire south-eastern coast of Nova Scotia, from Cape Sable to Cape Canso, a distance on a straight line of rather less than three hundred miles, would in this way constitute a bay, from which United States fishermen would be excluded.

The undersigned, however, forbears to dwell on this subject, being far from certain, on a comparison of all that is said in the two notes of Lord Aberdeen of the 10th instant, as to the relaxation proposed by her Majesty's government, that it is not intended to embrace the waters of the northeastern coasts of Cape Breton, as well as the Bay of Fundy.

Lord Aberdeen, towards the close of the note in which the purpose of her Majesty's government is communicated, invites the attention of the undersigned to the fact that British colonial fish is, at the present time, excluded by prohibitory duties from the markets of the United States, and suggests that the moment at which the British government are making a liberal concession to United States trade, might be deemed favorable for a counter concession on the part of the United States to British trade, by the reduction of duties which operate so prejudicially to the interests of British colonial fishermen.

The undersigned is of course without instructions which enable him to make any definite reply to this suggestion. It is no doubt true that the British colonial fish, as far as duties are concerned, enters the United States market, if at all, to some disadvantage. The government of the United States, he is persuaded, would gladly make any reduction in these duties which would not seriously injure the native fishermen; but Lord Aberdeen is aware that the encouragement of this class of the sea-faring community has ever been considered, as well in the United States as Great Britain, as resting on peculiar grounds of expediency. It is the great school not only of the commercial but of the public marine, and the highest considerations of national policy require it to be fostered.

The British colonial fishermen possess considerable advantages over those of the United States. The remoter fisheries of Newfoundland and Labrador are considerably more accessible to the colonial than to the United States fishermen. The fishing grounds on the coasts of New Brunswick and Nova Scotia, abounding in cod, mackerel and herring, lie at the doors of the former; he is therefore able to pursue his avocation in a smaller class of vessels, and requires a smaller outfit; he is able to use the net and the seine to great advantage in the small bays and inlets along the coast, from which the fishermen of the United States, under any construction of the treaty, are excluded. All or nearly all the materials of ship building, timber, iron, cordage and canvass are cheaper in the colonies than in the United States, as are salt, hooks and lines. There is also great advantage enjoyed in the former in reference to the supply of bait.

and curing the fish. These, and other causes, have enabled the colonial fishermen to drive those of the United States out of many foreign markets, and might do so at home but for the protection afforded by the duties.

It may be added that the highest duty on the kinds of fish that would be sent to the American market, is less than a half-penny per pound, which cannot do more than counter-balance the numerous advantages possessed by the colonial fishermen.

The undersigned supposes, though he has no particular information to that effect, that equal or higher duties exist in the colonies on the importation of fish from the United States.

The undersigned requests the earl of Aberdeen to accept the assurance of his high consideration.

EDWARD EVERETT.

Mr. Everett to Mr. Calhoun.

[No. 287.] LONDON, *April* 2, 1845.

SIR: I transmit herewith a note from Lord Aberdeen with sundry enclosures, relative to the seizure of the fishing vessel, the Argus, in the month of July last, together with a copy of my reply.

Although I do not think there is ground for charging those who complained of harsh treatment on the part of the captors of that vessel with intentional and malicious misrepresention, it is evident that their affidavits are quite inaccurate. It will be for the department to decide whether it will be expedient to call upon Messrs. J. & J. Starling, of Portland, the owners of the Argus, and the American consuls at Sydney and Halifax for further information.

Every case like this of exaggerated statement, and especially every complaint of ill-treatment where kindness has been experienced, is to be regretted not merely as morally wrong, but as tending unavoidably to impair the efficacy of official intervention to procure the redress of the wrongs of our citizens.

It is for this reason that I have been at more pains than would otherwise have been worth while, to point out to Lord Aberdeen the reasons which exist for thinking, that with considerable inaccuracies in their deposition, and a very unfortunate misstatement as to the participation of Mr. Dodd, the officer by whom they were captured, in the treatment complained of, there may not be in the substance of their narrative, sufficient reason to accuse them of a wilful departure from truth.

I am, sir, with great respect, your obedient servant,

EDWARD EVERETT.

[Enclosure.]

Lord Aberdeen to Mr. Everett.

FOREIGN OFFICE, *March* 10, 1845.

The undersigned, her Majesty's principal Secretary of State for Foreign Affairs, in his note of the 18th of October last, had the honor to inform

Mr. Everett, envoy extraordinary and minister plenipotentiary of the United States of America, that he had referred his note of the 9th of that month, and its enclosures respecting the "Argus" fishing vessel, to the colonial office, in order that inquiries might be made into that matter. Those inquiries having now been completed, the undersigned proceeds to make Mr. Everett acquainted with the result of them. The best mode of accomplishing this object will be by laying before Mr. Everett *in extenso* the whole of the papers relative to the case in question, which the undersigned has received from the colonial department, and which the undersigned has accordingly the honor to enclose herewith.

As the point of the construction of the convention of 1818 with reference to the rights of fishing on the coasts of the Anglo-American dependencies, by citizens of the United States, is treated in another note of the undersigned of this day's date, relative to the case of the Washington, the undersigned abstains from again touching upon that subject, and will confine himself in this note to the point of the harsh treatment of the patron and crew of the *Argus* by the commander of the Nova Scotia revenue cruiser *Sylph*, which is alleged in Mr. Everett's note of the 9th of October and its enclosures.

The undersigned must premise by observing that the affidavits of the parties who bring this charge against the commander of the *Sylph* are not only confused and obscure, but contradictory in themselves, and little calculated by their general tone to inspire confidence in the persons who make them. One of the parties, being one of the crew of the Argus, declares on oath that the capture of the Argus by the Sylph, took place on the 6th of July, while the other party, being equally one of the crew, declares on oath that the capture took place on the 9th of July. The capture did, in fact, take place on the 7th of August. These and other inaccuracies in the statements of the deponents show, to say the least of it, the light respect in which they must have held the obligation of an oath.

But Mr. Everett will moreover find, by a careful perusal of the letter addressed to Mr. Dodd by the collector of customs at Sydney, that the master of the Argus was not only not brought forward at all, but that he distinctly declared more than once to the collector that Mr. Dodd had treated him like a gentleman.

With regard to the general charge of harsh treatment brought against the commander of the "Sylph," by the two Doughtys, deponents, the undersigned may fearlessly refer Mr. Everett to Mr. Dodd's own declaration, supported as it is by that of Mr. Davenport, the collector of customs, already alluded to; and the undersigned has little doubt that a perusal of those papers will convince Mr. Everett that not only no harsh treatment was practised against the master and crew of the "Argus," but that they were treated, from first to last, with the utmost kindness and consideration. In fact, from Mr. Dodd's declaration, it clearly appears that nearly the whole of the affidavits of the two Doughtys, who depose against him, form a tissue of wilful and shameless misrepresentations; the more culpable because they exhibit the most flagrant ingratitude towards Mr. Dodd, who not only allowed them every indulgence, and stood between them and the collector of customs, in order to soften the rigor of the law, which the latter considered it his duty to carry into full effect, but, after the condemnation of their vessel, actually conveyed the master and two of his men, who were witnesses for him, to Halifax, in the "Sylph," at his (Mr. Dodd's) own expense, in consequence of having heard that they were anxious to proceed thither in the hope of obtaining the release of their vessel.

The undersigned apprehends that after taking cognizance of the papers to which he has referred, Mr. Everett will allow that there is no occasion for his adding one word to that evidence, in order to prove to Mr. Everett that this is a matter in which the whole of the facts have been grossly misrepresented by gratuitous malice, and that the interposition of the authority of the United States government, for the protection of the complainants, has been claimed on false pretences.

The undersigned has the honor to renew to Mr. Everett the assurances of his high consideration.

ABERDEEN.

[Enclosure.]

Downing Street, *January* 9, 1845.

My Lord: With reference to your lordship's letter of the 16th October, I am directed by Lord Stanley to transmit to you, for the information of the Earl of Aberdeen, the enclosed copy of a despatch which has been received from the Lieutenant Governor of Nova Scotia, relative to the seizure of the American fishing vessel Argus, which forms the subject of the note from the minister of the United States, enclosed in your above mentioned letter.

I have, &c., &c.,

JAMES STEPHEN.

Viscount Canning, &c., &c.

[Enclosure.]

Government House,
Halifax, December 17, 1844.

My Lord: I have the honor to acknowledge the receipt of your despatch, No. 191, of the 26th October, enclosing a letter from the minister of the United States of America at London, complaining of the "seizure of a vessel named the Argus, which was found fishing off Cape Breton under similar circumstances to those of the Washington, and stating that the captors had been harsh in their treatment towards the master of the Argus;" and likewise concerning depositions to that effect signed by Edward and Joshua Doughty.

After the correspondence I have lately had with your lordship as to the true construction to be put on the convention of 1818, on the interpretation of which the legality or illegality of the capture of the Argus as well as of the Washington, of course depends, I feel it is unnecessary for me to enter again on that branch of the subject; and from the difficulty of communication by post at this season of the year, I am not at present in a position to meet the allegations contained in Mr. Everett's representation with respect to the harsh treatment of the skipper and crew of the Argus by the captain and crew of the provincial schooner. These charges have, however, taken me by surprise, as William Doughty, the commander of the Argus, (and apparently, from the similarity of name, the brother of the other two men who feel themselves aggrieved,) was in Halifax some days, and in communication with the attorney general, to whom he made no complaint of having been ill-treated or harshly dealt with by Mr. Dodd, whose general character, as well as the kindly feeling he evinced towards William Doughty, forbids me readily to give credence to any accusation of such a nature that may be brought against him, until he shall have had an opportunity of offering a counter statement. I have, in consequence, transmitted to Mr. Dodd a copy of the affidavits of Edward and Joshua Doughty, and required an explanation from him, which I trust to receive in sufficient time to allow of my addressing your lordship satisfactorily on this topic by the next packet.

I have the honor, &c.,

FALKLAND.

Lord STANLEY, &c., &c.

DOWNING STREET, *January* 29, 1845.

MY LORD: With reference to my letter of the 9th instant I am directed by Lord Stanley to transmit to your lordship, for the information of the Earl of Aberdeen, the enclosed copy of a further despatch from the lieutenant governor of Nova Scotia, transmitting the answer of Mr. Dodd (the commander of the provincial revenue-schooner Sylph, at the time the American schooner Argus was captured by the former vessel) to the charge of harsh treatment towards the master and crew of the Argus, on the part of Mr. Dodd.

I have the honor, &c.,

G. W. HOPE.

Viscount CANNING, &c., &c.

GOVERNMENT HOUSE,
Halifax, January 2, 1845.

MY LORD: In accordance with the promise contained in my despatch No. 281, dated 17th December, 1844, I have the honor to enclose copies of a correspondence between the provincial secretary of Nova Scotia and Mr. Philip Dodd, the officer in command of the provincial revenue-schooner Sylph, at the time the American schooner Argus was captured by that vessel on the 6th of August last.

Mr. Dodd's letter is accompanied by a statement of Mr. Davenport, the collector of customs at Sydney, Cape Breton, which, taken with his own letter, appears to me, as I trust it will to your lordship, completely and satisfactorily to refute the charge of harsh treatment towards the master and crew of the Argus, on the part of Mr. Philip Dodd.

I think it right to remark that Edward and Joshua Doughty, who have preferred these charges, seem to have been simple mariners on board the Argus, of the same name as the commander, but not the skipper of that vessel, who is himself called William Doughty, and therefore, I hope, guiltless of the ingratitute which Mr. Dodd has attributed to him from similarity of name; but whether this be so or not, Mr. Dodd must, I think, be perfectly acquitted of having been harsh in his treatment of the fishermen of the United States who composed the crew of the Argus.

I have the honor, &c.,

FALKLAND.

Lord STANLEY, &c., &c.

PROVINCIAL SECRETARY'S OFFICE,
Halifax, December 13, 1844.

SIR: I have it in command from the lieutenant-governor to transmit to you the enclosed extract of a despatch which his Excellency has received from her Majesty's principal Secretary of State for the colonies, by which you will perceive that the minister of the United States at London has complained of the treatment which the master and crew of the American fishing vessel "Argus," lately seized by you, experienced from the captors,—and his Excellency is pleased to call upon you for a full explanation of your proceedings on the occasion in question, in order that her Majesty's government may be able to answer the complaint of the American minister, the substance of which is contained in the second accompanying paper.

I have, &c.,

RUPERT D. GEORGE.

PHILIP DODD, Esq.

SYDNEY, CAPE BRETON,
December 23, 1844.

SIR: I have the honor to acknowledge the receipt of your letter of the 13th instant with an extract of a despatch received by his Excellency, the lieutenant-governor from her Majesty's principal Secretary of State for the colonies, having reference to a charge against me as late commander of the revenue schooner Sylph, for harsh treatment to the master and crew of the American fishing vessel Argus seized by me, and requesting a full explanation of my proceedings on the occasion in question. In reply I have to state, for the information of his Excellency the lieutenant-governor, that when in command of the "Sylph" on the 6th of August last, then cruizing round the coast of Cape Breton, I discovered the Argus some miles off Saint Anne's with her crew actually employed fishing; and although more than three miles from any land, still much within the bay that is formed by a straight line drawn from Cape North to the northern head of Cow bay, and consequently I felt it my duty to take her into Sydney, being the nearest port to me at the time, at which an officer of her Majesty's customs was stationed. In corroboration of this part of my statement, I beg respectfully to refer to the affidavits made by two disinterested persons on board the "Sylph" at the time of seizure, at present in the office of the attorney-general at Halifax, and which I would now have renewed for the purpose of accompanying this communication, but the persons making them are out of the island of Cape Breton, and consequently out of my reach.

The fact of the owners of the Argus allowing her to be condemned in the admiralty court of Halifax, without a defence of any kind whatever, must, to most minds, carry a conviction that the vessel when seized was not within the limits in which subjects of the United States are permitted to fish on the coasts of this province. Had it been otherwise, as stated in the affidavit of Doughty, that the vessel was three miles outside the line before referred to,—how is it that a defence was not made to the action, and the important fact at least attempted to be proved, which if successful, would have liberated the vessel and cargo, and made me liable to an action for damages? But all on board the Argus were too well satisfied of their liability, and of theirhaving violated the treaty which excludes them from our shores, to have risked the test of an examination, as witnesses in the case, and therefore they abandoned a defence as hopeless. The vessel, as I have already stated, was brought into the harbor of Sydney, which was on the seventh, in the morning, when I gave her in charge, agreeably to my instructions, to the collector of customs at the port, whose letter to me of this day's date, herewith enclosed, I beg to refer to for a more detailed account and perfect confutation of the charge of harsh treatment by me towards the master and crew of the "Argus."

The "Argus," on coming into the harbor of Sydney, was accompanied by another American fishing vessel, both in the employ of the same owners, for the purpose of giving assistance to the crew of the "Argus." They had also the advice and assistance of the American consul stationed at the port of Sydney, and yet, with all this assistance at hand, I was most desirous of doing all in my power to make their situation as comfortable as the circumstances of their case would permit; and after their remaining on board the "Argus" full thirty hours from their arrival in Sydney, thus giving them every opportunity to collect their private property and be prepared to quit the vessel; still, at the expiration of that time, I called with Doughty, the master, upon the collector of the customs, and requested him to permit their remaining a further time on board, but which he declined, for the reasons stated in his letter before referred to. I have every reason for believing that no part of their clothing or private property was detained from them; for if such had been the case I am convinced Doughty would have mentioned the subject to me; and as to my being privy to such an act, I am satisfied never once came across the master's mind until instigated to make this base charge long after leaving Cape Breton, for up to the period of his parting with me in Halifax, he repeatedly, in the presence of others, thanked me for my kind treatment of himself and crew, and the same sentiments he must have expressed to his consul at Sydney, who also thanked me for what he was pleased to call my generous conduct towards them. Several days after the "Argus" had been in charge of the collector of the customs, and I was preparing to leave with the "Sylph" for Halifax, I discovered that Doughty, with two of his crew who were witnesses for him, were anxious to proceed there, with the hope of obtaining a release of the "Argus." Upon representing this to his Excellency, the Lieutenant Governor, and there being no other vessel in port at the time in which they could obtain a passage to Halifax, I, without a request on their part, offered them a passage in the "Sylph," and actually took them there without their being at any expense whatever. From the affidavit of Doughty being so completely at variance with truth I cannot help thinking he never could have supposed I would be called upon to answer it, for he knew full well how readily and perfectly his charge could be disproved; and were the consul of the United States still in Sydney, I would have no hesitation in being bound by a representation of the case as given to him by Doughty and his crew, together with what he himself witnessed of my conduct towards them; but that gentleman is now in Newfoundland, and I am therefore unable to obtain from him any corroboration of what I have now stated, but which, on his return to Cape Breton, I am quite satisfied can, if required, be procured. After the gross misrepresentation of Doughty, every line of his affidavit being marked with falsehood, it would almost induce me, should I again be honored with the command of one of the provincial revenue vessels, not to go out of my way for the mere purpose of extending to the class of persons to which Mr. Doughty belongs those acts of kindness and courtesy with which he was favored, but which have been returned by the blackest ingratitude.

I have, &c.,

P. S. DODD.

Sir RUPERT D. GEORGE, Bart., &c., &c., &c.

CUSTOM-HOUSE, *Sydney, December* 23, 1844.

SIR: I beg to state with reference to the complaint of Doughty, late master of the United States schooner 'Argus,' that on the afternoon of the day on which that vessel was placed in custody of the customs, having occasion to go into the town, I met two seamen in conversation with a gentleman, to whom, in very excited language, they were telling the story of that vessel's capture, and asserting that you had been guilty of great harshness to the crew.

I was at once referred to as the proper person to whom any complaint should be made, and then asked the man who he was and what he knew of the affair. He said he was the master of a fishing schooner belonging to the same owners as the 'Argus;' that he had been fishing in company with her, concealed by a fog bank at the time of the 'Argus's' seizure; that having learned she had been captured by the Sylph, he thought it right to come to Sydney and render the crew of the Argus any assistance that they might require. As you were not then in town, I did not communicate with you on the subject, but on the following morning Doughty was sent for to attend at the custom-house, and I then related to him the rumor circulated by the master of the other craft, and closely examined as to the truth of such and of all the circumstances connected with the seizure. He then expressed very strong feelings of indignation at the baseness of the authors of any report prejudicial to you. He assured me that no fault whatever could be found either with you or the Sylph's people, and twice or thrice repeated to me, "Mr. Dodd has behaved to us like a gentleman." At this moment, the man's earnestness of manner and these expressions, are most vividly impressed on my recollection.

To weigh the degree of accuracy which may be supposed to attach to the other assertions made by Doughty, I will remind you that it was on the morning of the 7th August, (not July as stated in the affidavit) that the Argus was placed in charge, the crew were not interfered with on that day, but were instructed to place themselves in communication with the United States consul; but on the day following the usual inventory was taken of the vessel's cargo, stores, sails, rigging, anchors, cables, and general fittings; and having given a receipt to you for these (a copy being also offered the master) I (not you as stated in the affidavit) desired the waiter and searcher of the port to request the personal baggage of the crew should then be removed, as the vessel required to be anchored in the stream, to prevent her being damaged as she must be where she then lay; the waiter at the same time offered the Queen's warehouse for the temporary reception of the baggage. After I had given this order, you may probably recollect bringing the master up to the custom-house and joining him in an application to allow the crew to remain on board the Argus, and the reasons I assigned for refusing these were: First, that having given a receipt to you and also to Doughty I had become personally responsible for all the goods named in the inventory; that in a former case the Hero, of Eastport, seized in 1838, under similar circumstances the crew had been thus billeted on the vessel and took away everything movable, for which I was of course accountable, and Doughty himself said he would expect everything returned to him in case of release. Secondly, because there was no reason why the regular course of procedure in all similar cases should be deviated from. The Argus crew had the means of immediate transport home in the sister craft, whose master had reported to me he came into port to render any assistance they might require. Besides, the consul was on the spot to provide all requisites, and there were ample means of shipping to the States. No less than thirteen vessels, British and United States, were loading for ports in the Union at that very time, and also as the Sylph must immediately resume her cruize, I did not think it prudent to allow a foreign prize to continue in charge of her own hostile crew, with a sister ship lying alongside ready to render any assistance required in a recapture, very easily effected, the Sylph once again at sea.

The crew of the Argus remained on board that vessel from the time she was brought into port, the night of the 7th August to about mid-day of the 8th, and therefore the story about their removal in fifteen minutes is not correct, and not less inaccurate is Doughty's assertion that the crew were denied any of their personal effects, because, later on the 9th than the events I have narrated, Doughty again applied at the custom-house for a hat said to have been left behind, the Argus being then removed to her final anchorage. I gave him an order to the ship keeper to give up the hat, and everything belonging to the master and crew, some of whom subsequently brought the hat on shore, together with some articles of cabin use, omitted in taking the inventory. This is a simple narrative of the facts.

I am, &c.,

HENRY DAVENPORT,
Collector.

P. S. Dodd, Esq., &c., &c., &c.

Mr. Everett to Lord Aberdeen.

Grosvenor Place, *April* 2, 1845.

The undersigned, envoy extraordinary and minister plenipotentiary of the United States of America, has had the honor to receive a note of the 10th instant, from the Earl of Aberdeen, her Majesty's principal Secretary of State for foreign affairs, in reply to the note of the undersigned of the 9th of October last, relative to the case of the United States fishing vessel, the "Argus," seized on the 6th of July last, off the north-eastern coast of Cape Breton by the provincial armed vessel the "Sylph."

In the above mentioned note of the 9th of October, after alluding very briefly to the alleged harsh treatment of the master and crew of the "Argus" by the captors, and adverting to the general subject of the contested right of the fishermen of the United States, in the waters of the Anglo-American provinces, the undersigned dwelt with all the earnestness in his power on the extremely objectionable character of the course pursued by the provincial authorities in presuming to decide for themselves a question under discussion between the two governments.

Of the often repeated complaints of the government of the United States on this point, a subject distinct from the general question as to the limits of the fishing privilege secured by the convention of 1818, to the people of the United States, no notice has been taken in any communication of Lord Aberdeen to the undersigned.

In reference to the complaint of "harsh treatment" in the case of the "Argus," the undersigned hastens to do an act of justice to the master of that vessel, by observing that it was through the inadvertence of the undersigned, that this complaint was said to be made in the deposition of "the late commander of the vessel." The letter of the American consul at Halifax, a copy of which accompanied the note of the undersigned of the 9th of October, mentions a deposition of the master; and this circumstance with the similarity of the name, led the undersigned to the too hasty conclusion, that one of the affidavits forwarded to him from Washington, and by him transmitted to Lord Aberdeen, was the deposition in question. Such, however, is not the case. The depositions accompanying the note of the undersigned, are those of two of the crew, sons of the master, one of them a boy of fourteen. The Earl of Aberdeen will perceive from Lord Folkland's letter of the 2d of January, that his lordship had conjectured that such was the fact, and was consequently disposed to exonerate William Doughty, the master of the vessel, from the charge of ingratitude, and of having made a deposition at home at variance with his professions of thankfulness both at Sydney and Halifax.

It does not appear that Captain Doughty had returned home at the time that Messrs. J. and J. Starling, of Portland, in Maine, the owners of the "Argus," represented the case to the Department of State at Washington.

With respect to the depositions of Edward and Joshua Doughty, the undersigned agrees with Lord Aberdeen that they are "confused and obscure," and that they are in some important particulars inaccurate, and he has much pleasure in adding that Mr. Dodd, the commander of the "Sylph," so far from treating the crew of the "Argus" with harshness, seems to have manifested to them every possible kindness consistent with the performance of his duty, as an officer charged with the execution of the provincial law.

But although the depositions of the Doughtys are materially incorrect, the undersigned is inclined to think them not open to the charge of intentional falsehood, wilful and shameless misrepresentation, and gratuitous malice ascribed to them by Mr. Dodd with the sanction of Lord Aberdeen. The statements for instance of Edward Doughty that the capture of the "Argus" took place on the 6th of July, and of Joshua Doughty that it took place on the 9th of July, to which Lord Aberdeen alludes as a contradiction showing a light respect to the obligation of an oath, are, the undersigned thinks, hardly sufficient ground for so heavy an imputation. The capture having taking place on the 6th of August, (not the 7th as stated by Lord Aberdeen,) both the depositions are in that respect of course inaccurate; but it is in a point of no prejudice to the captors, nor benefit to the deponents or their cause. Had they combined to swear to a false account, they would not have differed in details of this kind, nor would they have assigned a wrong day to the capture. The deposition was sent to the undersigned not in the original, but in a copy apparently written in haste and containing, either for that reason or the rapidity with which it was taken down before the magistrate, several clerical errors. The undersigned is disposed to think that the words "on the ninth" in the deposition of Joshua Doughty should read "in the month." This would remove the only point of contradiction between the brothers, and leave no error in reference to the date, but that of "July" for "August," an error for which the undersigned is unable to account, but which from its nature cannot well be other than inadvertent.

The report of Mr. Davenport, the collector, is itself not wholly free from contradiction in some important points. He observes in the earlier portion of it that the Argus was brought into Sydney in the morning of the seventh of August as was the fact, but in the last paragraph he says that this took place on the night of the seventh; and after having detailed at length in the body of his statement the transactions of the 8th instant, he adverts in its conclusion to an incident which, as he says, took place "later on the 9th than the events I have narrated." The undersigned by no means points out these errors for the sake of impeaching the general character of Mr. Davenport's statement, but to show that similar errors on the part of the Doughtys are not conclusive proof of wilful misrepresentation and falsehood.

As far as Mr. Dodd's conduct is concerned, the greatest inaccuracy of the deposition of the Doughtys consists in ascribing to him what was done by order of Mr. Davenport, the collector of Sydney. It appears by Mr. Davenport's statement that these orders were not given by him in person, but by a "waiter or searcher." The undersigned thinks that it is very much the custom of officers of this class in delivering orders not to describe very particularly from what superior functionary the orders emanate; and it seems natural that these uninformed fishermen, the Doughtys, might have supposed that the orders brought them to quit their vessel and the prohibition to remove any of her stores with them, proceeded from the officer by whom the capture was made. The undersigned sees no bad motive which they could have had in ascribing to Mr. Dodd what was done by Mr. Davenport. Their doing so may argue ignorance and carelessness, but not necessary malice.

It is worthy of remark that Mr. Dodd does not, with one exception, seem to discredit the statement of the Doughtys as to what took place before there was any opportunity to fall into this confusion, that is, after the capture and before the bringing into port, although that portion of their statement contains a report of Mr. Dodd's observations about what is called the "annexation document," and his having seized the vessel in order to settle a question under a treaty, which if incorrectly alleged, it may be thought he could hardly have failed to contradict. Mr. Dodd states, indeed, that it was impossible that the master of the Argus as asserted by the deponents, could have thought himself outside the line drawn from Cape North to the head of Cow bay, because if he had so thought he would have gone to trial against the captors at Halifax. But Lord Aberdeen is aware that it is one of the grievances which the government of the United States has had repeatedly to complain of, and which was prominently brought forward in connection with this very capture by the undersigned in his letter of the 9th of October, that no defence can be made in such a suit without giving security in $300, besides encountering the delay and the heavy expenses of court. After adverting to this fact, the consul at Halifax in his letter of 19th August, which was sent by the undersigned to Lord Aberdeen with his note of 9th October, adds, "so that, generally speaking, it is better to let the suit go by default and purchase the vessel after condemnation."

Mr. Dodd on this subject proceeds to say, that "all on board the Argus were too well satisfied of their liability and of their having violated the treaty which excludes them from our shores, to have asked the test of an examination as witnesses in the case, and therefore they abandoned the attempt as useless." But not to dwell on the circumstance that Mr. Dodd himself opposes no specific contradiction to the assertion of the Doughtys that he stated that he made the capture "to settle the question" as to the construction of the treaty, it is not to be conceived that he should be so uninformed on this subject as not to know that not merely on the part of the fishermen as a body, but on that of their government, the validity of the British construction of the treaty has always been contested, and that if the fishermen of the United States forbear to act on the construction which their own government has ever maintained, it is simply to avoid capture by the provincial armed vessels.

Admitting that the Doughtys may innocently have thought that the orders which were brought by "the searcher" proceeded not from the collector but from the officer who captured the vessel, the undersigned does not find in this statement itself much further discrepancy from the admissions of Mr. Davenport, than may always be expected between the representations of an officer of intelligence justifying his conduct to his superiors, and those of ignorant men telling their story to their employers under a strong sense of recent loss and oppression.

Mr. Davenport in one point makes a charge against the Doughtys for which there is no foundation in their narrative. He says, "the crew of the Argus remained on board that vessel from the time she was brought into port, the night of the 7th of August to about mid-day of the 8th, and therefore the story about their removal in fifteen minutes is not correct." But the Doughtys expressly mention that the crew of the Argus remained on board from the time the vessel was brought in on the morning of the 7th till ten o'clock of the 8th. The "fifteen minutes" ran from the time the order was given to leave the vessel, not from their arrival in port, and without any reference to the deposition of the Doughtys, the undersigned would infer from the statement of the collector himself, that after the inventory was taken on the morning of the 8th, the crew were peremptorily required to quit the vessel; and as her "stores" were included in the inventory, it is equally plain that they were not permitted to carry the means of subsistence away with them. It appears from his own report that Mr. Davenport, even when urged to do so by Mr. Dodd, refused to relax in any degree the rigor of the law towards those whom he thinks proper to designate as the hostile crew of the Argus.

The conduct of Mr. Dodd, in endeavoring to procure from the collector permission for these poor fishermen to stay on board their *own* vessel another day, (for it must be remembered she was not yet judicially proceeded against, and that therefore in the humane intendment of the law her master was as yet innocent of its violation,) was certainly kind, and his furnishing, unsolicited, a gratuitous passage to Halifax for the captain of the Argus and two of his crew, still more so; although this was not done, as Lord Aberdeen appears to be under the impression, "after the condemnation of the vessel," but before the commencement of any judicial proceeding against her. It was, however, not the less meritorious, and the undersigned sincerely regrets the injustice done him in the deposition of the Doughtys. Could he now deem that injustice wilful, or should it on further inquiry so appear, the undersigned would not fall behind Lord Aberdeen in his emphatic reprobation of it.

The undersigned hopes, however, that the foregoing suggestions will lead Lord Aberdeen to a judgment somewhat more favorable on that point. That the depositions of the Doughtys were given under feelings of great irritation is quite evident. This furnishes no excuse for exaggeration and mis-statement; still less does it palliate falsehood and perjury. Of these crimes the undersigned is inclined to think them innocent; and Lord Aberdeen will agree with him in regarding some coloring in statements made under imaginary wrong, as almost inseparable from human frailty.

In this case the undersigned is constrained to add that in the judgment of the government of the United States the wrong was real and extreme, not in the harsh treatment on the part of the capturing officer, (a charge against Mr. Dodd to which no prominence was originally given by the undersigned, which he has much pleasure in abandoning, and should have had none in being able to substantiate,) but in the essential injustice of the colonial law, which that gentleman and the collector were employed in enforcing. It cannot need an argument to show that while a question is in discussion between her Majesty's government and that of the United States, and is even, as appears by Lord Aberdeen's note to the undersigned, under reference to legal authorities, an enactment of the provincial legislature purporting to decide said question to themselves, and enforcing that desision by capture and condemnation, possesses none of the qualities of the law of civilized States but its forms.

The undersigned sincerely hopes that he has not erred in believing that the recent determination of her Majesty's government, communicated by a separate note of Lord Aberdeen of the 10th instant, may be intended to receive such a construction as will furnish a final and effectual remedy of this grievance.

The undersigned requests the Earl of Aberdeen to accept the assurance of his high consideration.

EDWARD EVERETT.

Mr. Everett to Mr. Buchanan.

[No. 305.] LONDON, *April* 23, 1845.

SIR: With my despatch, No. 278, of 25th March, I transmitted the note of Lord Aberdeen, of the 10th of March, communicating the important information that this government had come to the determination to concede to American fishermen the right of pursuing their occupation within the Bay of Fundy. It was left somewhat uncertain by Lord Aberdeen's note whether this concession was intended to be confined to the Bay of Fundy, or to extend to other portions of the coast of the Anglo-American possessions, to which the principles contended for by the government of the United States, equally apply, and particularly to the waters on the north-eastern shores of Cape Breton, where the "Argus" was captured. In my notes of the 25th ultimo and 2d instant, on the subject of the "Washington" and the "Argus," I was careful to point out to Lord Aberdeen that all the reasons for admitting the right of Americans to fish in the Bay of Fundy, apply to those waters, and with superior force, inasmuch as they are less landlocked than the Bay of Fundy, and to express the hope that the concession was meant to extend to them, which there was some reason to think, from the mode in which Lord Aberdeen expressed himself, was the case.

I received last evening, the answer of his lordship, informing me that my two notes had been referred to the colonial office, and that a final reply could not be returned till he should be made acquainted with the result of that reference, and that, in the mean time, the concession must be understood to be limited to the Bay of Fundy.

The merits of the question are so clear that I cannot but anticipate that the decision of the colonial office will be in favor of the liberal construction of the convention. In the mean time I beg leave to suggest, that in any public notice which may be given that the Bay of Fundy is henceforth open to American fishermen, it should be carefully stated that the extension of the same privilege to the other great bays on the coasts of the Anglo-American dependencies, is a matter of negotiation between the two governments.

I am, sir, with great respect, your obedient servant,

EDWARD EVERETT.

JAMES BUCHANAN, Esq.
Secretary of State.

The Earl of Aberdeen to Mr. Everett.

FOREIGN OFFICE, *April* 21, 1845.

The undersigned, her Majesty's principal Secretary of State for Foreign Affairs, has the honor to acknowledge the receipt of the two notes which Mr. Everett, envoy extraordinary and minister plenipotentiary of the United States of America, addressed to him on the 25th ultimo and on the 2d instant, relative to the case of the Argus, and that of the Washington, United States' fishing vessels.

Those notes have been brought under the consideration of her Majesty's

Secretary of State for the colonies, and the undersigned postpones, therefore, replying to their contents, until he shall have become acquainted with the results of that reference.

In the meantime, however, the undersigned thinks it expedient to guard himself against the assumption of Mr. Everett, that it may have been his intention by his note of the 10th ultimo, to include other bays on the coasts of the British North American provinces, in the relaxation which he therein notified to Mr. Everett, as to be applied henceforward to the Bay of Fundy. That note was intended to refer to the Bay of Fundy alone.

The undersigned avails himself of this opportunity to renew to Mr. Everett the assurances of his high consideration.

ABERDEEN.

Mr. Buchanan to Mr. Bancroft.

[No. 5.]

DEPARTMENT OF STATE,
Washington, December 10, 1846.

SIR: I have the honor to transmit to you herewith, at the instance of the Hon. D. P. King, of the House of Representatives of the United States, certain orignal and other documents from the files of this office, relating to the cases of the American fishing schooners "Director," E. Haskell, master, and "Pallas," Job Denner, master, both of Rockport, Massachusetts.

These vessels were seized in the Gulf of St. Lawrence, in the autumn of 1840, by the British revenue cutter "John and Louisa Wallace," Stephens, master, for an alleged trespass upon British fishing grounds, carried into Nova Scotian ports, and ultimately, under circumstances set forth in the accompanying papers, wholly lost to their owners.

An examination of the records of the United States legation in London for some years past, will show you that cases of a similar character have not unfrequently occurred heretofore, and have formed the subject of complaints to the British government. It will also show you the result of these applications in behalf of the owners and others interested in American vessels engaged in the fisheries thus vexatiously seized by the British provincial authorities.

If, after a careful perusal and consideration of the correspondence referred to, and of the documents now sent, you shall be of opinion that the cases of the "Director" and "Pallas," or either of them, might now, under all the circumstances, be presented to the British government with a reasonable hope of a satisfactory decision on its part, you are authorized to invite Lord Palmerston's attention to them in such terms as you may judge best calculated to secure the ends of justice.

I am, sir, very respectfully, your obedient servant,

JAMES BUCHANAN.

GEORGE BANCROFT, Esq., &c., &c.

[Enclosure.]

HOUSE OF REPRESENTATIVES,
Washington, December 10, 1846.

SIR: Enclosed is a letter addressed to our minister at the court of St. James, and I avail myself of the permission given by you to ask that it may be forwarded with the instructions given to him in relation to the fishing vessels belonging to our citizens, which have been captured by British cruisers.

I have the honor to be, with great respect, your obedient servant,

DANIEL P. KING.

To the Hon. JAMES BUCHANAN,
Secretary of State.

[Extract.]

Mr. Bancroft to Mr. Buchanan.

LEGATION OF THE UNITED STATES,
London, January 4, 1847.

SIR: Your despatches Nos. 5 and 6 have come to hand. The last shall receive instant attention immediately on Lord Palmerston's return from the country. As it regards the claim for the fishing vessels taken in 1840, I am not so clear, and will write again on the subject after mature examination. Till then I shall exercise the discretion which you direct me to use.

I am, sir, very respectfully, your obedient servant,

GEORGE BANCROFT.

Mr. Crampton to Mr. Webster.

WASHINGTON, *July* 5, 1852.

SIR: I have been directed by her Majesty's government to bring to the knowledge of the government of the United States a measure which has been adopted by her Majesty's government to prevent a repetition of the complaints which have so frequently been made of the encroachments of vessels belonging to citizens of the United States and of France upon the fishing grounds reserved to Great Britain by the convention of 1818.

Urgent representations having been addressed to her Majesty's government by the governors of the British North American provinces in regard to these encroachments, whereby the colonial fisheries are most seriously prejudiced, directions have been given by the lords of her Majesty's admiralty for stationing off New Brunswick, Nova Scotia, Prince Edward's Island, and in the Gulf of St. Lawrence, such a force of small sailing vessels and steamers as shall be deemed sufficient to prevent the infraction of the treaty. It is the command of the Queen that the officers employed upon this service should be especially enjoined to avoid all interference with the vessels of friendly powers, except where they are in the act of violating the treaty, and on all occasions to avoid giving ground of complaint by the adoption of harsh or unnecessary proceedings when circumstances compel their arrest or seizure.

I avail myself of this opportunity to renew to you, sir, the assurance of my high consideration.

JOHN F. CRAMPTON.

Honorable DANIEL WEBSTER, &c., &c., &c.

Mr. Hunter to Mr. Crampton.

DEPARTMENT OF STATE,
Washington, July 14, 1852.

SIR: I have the honor to acknowledge the receipt of your note of the 5th instant, in which, by direction of your government, you bring to the knowledge of that of the United States, a measure which has been adopted by her Britannic Majesty's government to prevent a repetition of the complaints which have so frequently been made, of the encroachments of vessels belonging to the citizens of the United States and of France upon the fishing grounds reserved to Great Britain by the convention of 1818; and to be, with high, consideration, sir, your obedient servant,

W. HUNTER,
Acting Secretary.

JOHN F. CRAMPTON, Esq., &c.

www.ingramcontent.com/pod-product-compliance
Lightning Source LLC
LaVergne TN
LVHW021407110826
845150LV00007B/1826